T0278381

SELECTED AND NEW POEMS

John F. Deane was born on Achill Island, Co Mayo, Ireland. He is the founder of Poetry Ireland, the National Poetry Society, and *The Poetry Ireland Review*. He is founder of the Dedalus Press, of which he was editor from 1985 until 2006. In 2006 he was visiting scholar in the Burns Library of Boston College, and in 2016 was Teilhard de Chardin Fellow in Christian Studies, Loyola University, Chicago and taught a course in poetry. In 2019 he was visiting poet in Notre Dame University, Indiana. His poems have been translated into many languages and in 2022 the Polish Publisher, Znak, published his *Selected Poems* in Polish translation. Deane is the recipient of many awards for his poetry, he is a member of Aosdána, the body established by the Arts Council to honour artists 'whose work has made an outstanding contribution to the arts in Ireland'. In 2007 he was made *Chevalier en l'ordre des arts et des lettres* by the French Government. The fine arts press, Guillemot, Cornwall, in 2019 published a limited edition book, *Like the Dewfall* and in 2022 a further booklet, *Voix Celeste*, both with artwork by Tony Martin. In late 2022, Irish Pages Press published *Darkness Between Stars*, a selection of poems focusing on questions of faith and poetry by both John F. Deane and James Harpur, including an email dialogue on their individual writing processes.

Selected and New Poems

John F. Deane

CARCANET POETRY

Acknowledgements

Early Poems were taken from *Stalking After Time* (Profile Press 1977); *High Sacrifice* (Dolmen Press 1981); *Winter in Meath* (Dedalus Press 1985); *Road, with Cypress and Star* (Dedalus Press 1988); *Walking on Water* (Dedalus Press 1994); *Christ, with Urban Fox* (Dedalus Press 1997)

First published in Great Britain in 2023 by
Carcanet
Alliance House, 30 Cross Street
Manchester, M2 7AQ
www.carcanet.co.uk

Text copyright © John F. Deane 2023

The right of John F. Deane to be identified as the author
of this work has been asserted in accordance with the
Copyright, Design and Patents Act of 1988; all rights reserved.

A CIP catalogue record for this book is
available from the British Library.

ISBN 978 1 80017 359 0

Book design by Andrew Latimer, Carcanet
Typesetting by LiteBook Prepress Services
Printed in Great Britain by SRP Ltd, Exeter, Devon

The publisher acknowledges financial
assistance from Arts Council England.

Under the trees the fireflies
zip and go out, like galaxies;
our best poems, reaching in from the periphery,
are love poems, achieving calm.

On the road, the cries of a broken rabbit
were pitched high in their unknowing;
our vehicles grind the creatures down
till the child's tears are for all of us,

dearly beloved, ageing into pain,
and for herself, for what she has discovered
early, beyond this world's loveliness. Always
after the agitated moments, the search for calm.

Curlews scatter now on a winter field, their calls
small alleluias of survival; I offer you
poems, here where there is suffering and joy,
evening, and morning, the first day.

This gathering of work,
selected and new,
is dedicated to Ursula

CONTENTS

Early Poems

from *Toccata and Fugue*, New & Selected Poems (2000)

from *Manhandling the Deity* (2003)

from *The Instruments of Art* (2005)

from *A Little Book of Hours* (2008)

from *Eye of the Hare*, (2011)

from *Naming of the Bones* (2021)

SELECTED AND NEW POEMS

BASKING SHARK: ACHILL ISLAND

Where bogland hillocks hid a lake
we placed a tom-cat on a raft; our guns
clawed pellets in his flesh until, his back
arched, the pink tongue bitten through, he drowned.
We fished for gulls with hooks we'd hide
in bread and when they swallowed whole we'd pull;
screaming they sheared like kites above a wild
sea; twine broke and we forgot. Until
that day we swam where a great shark
glided past, dark and silent power
half-hidden through swollen water; stunned
we didn't shy one stone. Where seas lie calm
dive deep below the surface; silence there
pounds like panic and moist fingers touch.

ISLAND WOMAN

It wasn't just the building of a bridge,
for even before, they had gone by sea
to Westport and from there abroad, and each
child sent money home till death in the family
brought him, reluctant, back. Of course the island
grew rich and hard, looked, they say, like Cleveland.

On a bridge the traffic moves both ways.
My own sons went and came, their sons, and theirs;
each time, in the empty dawn, I used to pray
and I still do, for mothers. I was there
when the last great eagle fell in a ditch.
My breasts are warts. I never crossed the bridge.

GALLARUS

No gilded tabernacle here, staunch
in authority; the walls house gloom.
Who has set the sun in the heavens has withdrawn
into thick darkness. These stones are cold,

bones on a winter shore that have lost
a soul. Silence only. Heaven
and the highest heavens don't contain him
and will this tent once built by bones?

Beyond, the ocean grinds the old
questions, decay and resurrection,
and warm blood. Do I find answers
here? stone-cold inside this skull.

PENANCE

They leave their shoes, like signatures, below;
above, their God is waiting. Slowly they rise
along the mountainside where rains and winds go
hissing, slithering across. They are hauling up

the bits and pieces of their lives, infractions
of the petty laws, the little trespasses and
sad transgressions. But this bulked mountain
is not disturbed by their passing, by this mere

trafficking of shale, shifting of its smaller stones.
When they come down, feet blistered and sins
fretted away, their guilt remains and that black
mountain stands against darkness above them.

ON A DARK NIGHT

On a dark night
When all the street was hushed, you crept
Out of our bed and down the carpeted stair.
I stirred, unknowing that some light
Within you had gone out, and still I slept.
As if, out of the dark air

Of night, some call
Drew you, you moved in the silent street
Where cars were white with frost. Beyond the gate
You were your shadow on a garage-wall.
Mud on our laneway touched your naked feet.
The dying elms of our estate

Became your bower
And on your neck the chilling airs
Moved freely. I was not there when you kept
Such a hopeless tryst. At this most silent hour
You walked distracted with your heavy cares
On a dark night while I slept.

WINTER IN MEATH
i.m. Tomas Tranströmer

Again we have been surprised
deprived, as if suddenly,
of the earth's familiarity

it is like the snatching away of love
making you aware at last you loved

sorrows force their way in, and pain
like memories half contained

the small birds, testing boldness, leave
delicate tracks
            closer
to the back door

while the cherry flaunts blossoms of frost
and stands in desperate isolation

~

the base of the hedgerow is a cliff of snow
the field is a still of a choppy sea
white waves capped in a green spray

a grave was dug into that hard soil
and overnight the mound of earth
grew stiff and white as stones flung onto a beach

our midday ceremony was hurried, forced
hyacinths and holly wreaths dream birds
appearing on our horizonless ocean

~

the body sank slowly
the sea closed over
things on the seabed stirred
again in expectation

~

this is a terrible desolation

the word 'forever'
stilling all the air

to glass

~

night tosses and seethes;
mind and body chafed all day
as a mussel-boat restlessly irritates
the mooring

on estuary water a fisherman
drags a long rake against the tide; one
snap of a rope and boat and this
solitary man
sweep off together into night

perhaps the light from my window
will register a moment with some god
riding by on infrangible glory

~

at dawn
names of the dead
appear on the pane

beautiful

in undecipherable frost

breath
hurts them
and they fade

~

the sea has gone grey as the sky
and as violent

pier and jetty go under
again and again
as a people suffering losses

a flock of teal from the world's edge
moves low over the water
finding grip for their wings along the wind

already among stones
a man
        like a priest
stooping in black clothes
has begun beachcombing

the dead, gone silent in their graves
have learned the truth about resurrection

~

you can almost look into the sun
silver in the silver-blue monstrance
cold over the barren white cloth of the world

for nothing happens
each day is an endless waiting
for the freezing endlessness of the dark

once – as if you had come across
a photograph, or a scarf maybe – a silver
monoplane like a knife-blade cut
across the still and haughty sky

but the sky healed up again after the passing that left
only a faint, pink thread, like a scar

FRANCIS OF ASSISI 1182 : 1982

Summer has settled in again; ships,
softened to clouds, hang on the horizon;
buttercups, like bubbles, float
on fields of a silver-grey haze; and words
recur, such as light, the sea, and God

the frenzy of crowds jostling towards the sun
contains silence, as eyes contain
blindness; we say, may the Lord
turning his face towards you
give you peace

morning and afternoon the cars moved out
onto the beach and clustered, shimmering,
as silver herring do in a raised net; this
is a raucous canticle to the sun

altissimu, omnipotente, bon Signore

to set up flesh
in images of snow and of white
roses, to preach to the sea
on silence, to man
on love, is to strain towards death
as towards a body without flaw

our poems, too, are gestures of a faith
that words of an undying love
may not be without some substance

words hovered like larks above his head, dropped
like blood from his ruptured hands

tue so'le laude, et onne benedictione

we play, like children, awed and hesitant
at the ocean's edge;
between dusk and dark the sea
as if it were God's long and reaching fingers
appropriates each footprint from the sand

I write down words, such as light, the sea, and God
and a bell rides out across the fields
like a man on a horse with helmet and lance
gesturing foolishly towards night

laudato si, Signore, per sora nostra
morte corporale

at night, the cars project
ballets of brightness and shadow on the trees
and pass, pursuing
darkness at the end of their tunnels of light

the restful voices have been swept by time
beyond that storybook night sky
where silence
drowns them out totally

ON STRAND ROAD
for Seamus Heaney

Waves have been sweeping in over the sandflats
under a chilling breeze; there is a man
windsurfing, stooping like a steeplejack
into his task; the summer girls who ran

with long gandering strides over the sand
are ghosts within a book. The poet's window
looks out across the sea towards England
and the cold north; like his bird he has grown

fabulous, comes down at times to touch
the range wall for conviction. The man on the sea
relishes each crest and hollow, and each
bow bend starts out on another journey.

GHOST

I sat where she had sat
in the fireside chair
expecting her to come down the stairs
into the kitchen;

the door was open, welcoming,
coals shifted in the Rayburn,
a kettle hummed;
she heard the susurrations of the fridge.

She had surrounded herself with photographs,
old calendars, hand-coloured picture-postcards;
sometimes a robin looked in at her from the world
or a dog barked vacantly from the hill;

widowed she sat, in the fireside chair,
leaning into a populated past;
she sat so quietly, expecting ghosts,
that a grey mouse moved by, uncurious,

till she stomped her foot against the floor;
and did she sense, I wondered, the ghost
who would come after her death to sit
where she had sat, in the fireside chair?

ARTIST

This was the given image –
a moulded man-body
elongated into pain, the head
sunk in abandonment: the cross.

I see it now
as the ultimate in ecstasy,
attention focused, the final words
rehearsed; there are black

nail-heads and contrasting
plashes of blood
like painter's oils: self-portrait
with grief and darkening sky;

something like Hopkins,
our intent, depressive scholar
who gnawed on the knuckle-bones of words
for sustenance – because God

scorched his bones with nearness
so that he cried with a loud voice
out of the entangling, thorny
underbrush of language.

CHRIST, WITH URBAN FOX

I

He was always there for our obeisance,
simple, ridiculous,
not sly, not fox, up-front – whatever,
man-God, God-man, Christ – but there.
Dreadlocks almost, and girlish, a beard
trim in fashion, his feminine
fingers pointing to a perfect
heart chained round with thorns;
his closed and slim-fine lips
inveigling us towards pain.

II

Did he know his future? while his blood
slicked hotly down the timbers did he know
the great hasped rock of the tomb
would open easily as a book of poems
breathing the words out? If he knew
then his affliction is charade, as is our hope;
if he was ignorant – his mind, like ours,
vibrating with upset – then his embrace of pain
is foolishness beyond thought, and there –
where we follow, clutching to the texts –
rests our trust, silent, wide-eyed, appalled.

III

I heard my child scream out
in pain on her hospital bed,
her eyes towards me where I stood
clenched in my distress;

starched sheets, night-lights, night-fevers,
soft wistful cries of pain,
long tunnel corridors down which flesh
lies livid against the bone.

IV

Look at him now, this king of beasts, grown
secretive before our bully-boy modernity,
master-shadow among night-shadows,
skulking through our wastes. I watched a fox
being tossed under car wheels, thrown like dust
and rising out of dust, howling in its agony;
this is not praise, it is obedience,
the way the moon suffers its existence,
the sky its seasons. Man-God, God-man, Christ,
suburban scavenger – he has danced
the awful dance, the blood-jig, has been strung
up as warning to us all, his snout
nudging still at the roots of intellect.

THE FOX-GOD

Across the fields and ditches, across the unbridgeable
mean width of darkness, a fox barked out its agony;
all night it fretted, whimpering like a famished child,

and the rain fell without pity; it chewed at its flesh,
gnawed on its bared bone, until, near dawn, it died.
The fox, they will say, is vermin, and its god

a vermin god, it will not know, poor creature,
how it is suffering – it is yourself you grieve for.
While I, being still a lover of angels, demanding

a Jacob's ladder beyond our fields, breathed
may El Shaddai console you into that darkness.
I know there was no consolation. No fox-god came.

But at dawn, man the enemy came, stalking fields,
snares in his bag, a shotgun cocked. Poor
creatures. The gap out of life, we have learned,

is fenced over with affliction. We, too, some dusk,
will take a stone for pillow, we will lie down, snared,
on the uncaring earth. Poor creatures. Poor creatures.

FATHER

'This is the way towards kindness'
he said, 'believe me', and I did;
I saw the small brown flecks of wisdom
like rust-drops on his hands;
six blind, sleek, mewling kittens

birth-wet and innocent of claw
he gathered into a hessian bag
with stones for travelling companions
and swung and swung it through the blue air
and out into the waters of the lake.

Sometimes still I see them scrabbling,
their snout-heads raised, their bodies
nude and shivering in an alien element,
sometimes – when I see the children,
their big, wide-open eyes unseeing,

skin stretched dry and crinkling
like leather and above them the blue sky,
that enviable sun shining – again I hear
'this is the way towards kindness,
believe me' and I do, I do, I do.

SILENCE

I was watching for the flight past
of a comet that would not pass again
for over a thousand years; I saw

only the stars and once the steady
unremarkable progress of some
man-made scrap-heap drifting across the sky;

but I was satisfied, awed once more
by the unaccountable night.
Somewhere in earth-darkness a dog

barked and fell silent. I inhaled
stars and quiet and my own minuscule standing
on the rim of the world, how the silence

that stretched before the music of the spheres
would have been an orchestra tuning up,
a strife of instruments before the symphony's great

knock-on-the-door, or how the prolonged
vegetable and animal quiet utterly failed
when a human voice screamed from behind a hill.

A REAL PRESENCE

I came out into pre-dawn darkness;
a fine rain was falling through the amber
aura of the street-lamps;

here in the suburbs we expect no cock-crow,
lights will come on in bath- or bed-room, lives
plugged in again, switched on;

the rubbish has been set out, uncertain
sentinel at each front-garden wall;
we were beginning to suspect an interloper –

black plastic sacks ripped open identifying
a brute invisible hunger, some real presence
disturbing to us. I stood awhile, perplexed;

this is not how I had envisaged it, these
sedulous rows of houses, tarmacadam lawns,
as if the words I'd learnt had slewed away

from what they named, the way my flesh
has lost intercourse with the hard earth;
and then I saw it, beautiful beast body

slipping like memory across unsociable darkness;
'fox', I whispered, 'fox';
it saw me, too, we touched a moment

until it turned, disdainfully, and I heard the soft
pat pat pat on the concrete of its proud withdrawal
down the street, around a corner; it disappeared

and left me thrilling, as if to name it were enough
to have everything back in place, the hedgerows,
immanence, survival, the eternal laws.

THE JOURNEY

Should you then, at the threshold,
stumble and cry out, leaving behind you
the ones you love, should you have
bathed your face in the cold water
that brings you from the deep out into morning,
and should you then in the sky find tears –
flight dividing the waters from the waters,
the sea beneath you smooth as lawns –
you are learning again how you are froth
on the ocean, a bone-chip out of genesis,
how you are shiftful a while but urgent always
for the wafting of waters that will carry you
back at last to the same door,
the old threshold, the glad step upwards.

OFFICIUM

Spare me Lord for my days burn off like dew.
What is man that you should magnify him;
why do you tender towards him your heart of love?
You visit him at dawn, touching him with dreams,
whisper to him at dusk, while the swings still shift
and soft rain falls on the abandoned frames.
Why have you made him contrary to you
that he learn baseness, anger and defeat
swallowing his own saliva in sudden dread?
Can you erase his sins, like chalk-marks,
or place your angels as a fence about him?
The trees dreep softly, the attendants are gone home.
Today I will lie down in sand, and if tomorrow
you come in search of me, I am no more.

FRENZY

A small row-boat on Keel Lake,
the water sluppering gently as he rowed,
the easy sh-sh-sshhhh of the reeds

as we drifted in, and all about us
tufts of bog-cotton like white moths,
the breathing heathers, that green-easy lift

into the slopes of Slievemore. All else
the silence of islands, and the awe
of small things wonderful: son,

father, on the one keel, the ripples
lazy and the surfaces of things unbroken.
Then the prideful swish of his line

fly-fishing, the curved rod graceful,
till suddenly may-fly were everywhere,
small water-coloured shapes like tissue,

sweet as the host to trout and – by Jove!
he whispered, old man astounded again
at the frenzy that is in all living.

NIGHTWATCH

In our suburban villages, our dormitory towns
we lie secure. But at the city's core
up and down the crack-tiled steps of the men's
shelter, they pass who could be minister

or president or priest – but are not;
in dust-striped suits and mismatched waistcoats
who could be civil servants – but are not;
greased and creased and ill-at-ease they ghost,

side-staggering, our streets, who might
be Plato, Luther, Hopkins but for some tiny thing
that slipped and shifted them a little to the side.
Their dream is a coin found under slanting

light, oblivion enough to damp down care
a while. But wish us all good health and reason
who wake sometimes, knowing we too have been
visited by importunate ghosts and have forgotten;

tell us what we dreamed, interpret for us the dream.

ACOLYTE

The wildness of this night – the summer trees
ripped and letting fall their still green leaves,
and the sea battering the coast
in its huge compulsion – seems as nothing

to the midnight chime from the black tower,
reiterating that all this tumult
is but the bones of Jesus in their incarnation.
I have flown today onto the island,

our small plane tossed like jetsam on the clouds;
I watched the girl, her mutilated brain,
the father urging, how her body rocked
in unmanageable distress, her fingers

bruising a half-forgotten doll; hers, too,
the Jesus-body, the Jesus-bones. Once
in early morning, the congregation
was an old woman coughing against echoes

and a fly frantic against the high window;
the words the priest used were spoken out as if
they were frangible crystal : *hoc - est – enim…*
The Host was a sunrise out of liver-spotted hands

and I tinkled the bell with a tiny gladness;
the woman's tongue was ripped, her chin,
where I held the paten, had a growth of hairs;
her breath was fetid and the Host balanced

a moment, and fell. Acolyte I gathered
up the Deity, the perfect white of the bread
tinged where her tongue had tipped it; the
necessary God, the beautiful, the patience.

I swallowed it, taking within me
Godhead and congregation, the long obedience
of the earth's bones, and the hopeless urge
to lay my hands in solace on the world.

Gotland, July 2000

CANTICLE

Sometimes when you walk down to the red gate
hearing the scrape-music of your shoes across gravel,
a yellow moon will lift over the hill;
you swing the gate shut and lean on the topmost bar
as if something has been accomplished in the world;
a night wind mistles through the poplar leaves
and all the noise of the universe stills
to an oboe hum, the given note of a perfect
music; there is a vast sky wholly dedicated
to the stars and you know, with certainty,
that all the dead are out, up there, in one
holiday flotilla, and that they celebrate
the fact of a red gate and a yellow moon
that tunes their instruments with you to the symphony.

LATE OCTOBER EVENING

We sat and watched the darkness close
– like a slow galleon under black sail
nearing; and grew conscious again of those
of our loved dead who might come, pale

in their murmuring group, up the long road
towards us. Thrush and blackbird hurled
valiant songs against the gloom as though
this was the first dying of the world.

You and I drew closer still
in the fire's glow, grateful this far
for love and friendship, while the low hill
melded with the dark and a perfect star

swung on its shoulder. When I turned back,
near sleep, to hold you, I could pray
our dead content again under black
sails, the tide brimming, then falling away.

And did you catch it then? that offered flash
of brilliance across the gloom? there by a curve
of the river, by the salleys and ash-trees, a brash
iridescence of emerald and blue —
kingfisher! Skulking you were, and sulking, astray
from sacrament and host, with your dreary
dwelling on the ego. Pathetic. Pray
grace in that sacred presentation, the high
shock of what is beautiful leading you to betray
this self-infusion for a while. And then that cry —
its piping *chee-chee-chee*, secretive by the stream's drift
and you step closer, cautiously, grace being still
easily squandered, till you have it before you: the gift!
loveliness, and a dagger-like poised bill.

THE MEADOWS OF ASPHODEL

The gate leans crookedly and blue binding-twine
clamps it against strays. Over peat acres
bog-cotton sways like a chorus of souls arrayed

for paradise, prepared to utter into praise.
In this humped meadow the individual graves
are clothed in dogrose and montbretia, clumps

of soiled-white lilies and the tut-tut-tutting
wheatears. Neglect, I say, and you say
repose, how the dead have abandoned us, become

seeds curled in darkness, their only task to wait
the nourishment and ripening; here it is the living
are blown about by the winds. The stones

with their weathering, their burthen of names
and aspirations, face, you say, all in the same
direction, and I say, East, waiting

for that disturbance, the grincing of the gate
when we will all stir out of repose, and lift, prepared
for counting, like pale down shivering before the breeze.

THE INSTRUMENTS OF ART
(Edvard Munch)

We move in draughty, barn-like spaces, swallows
busy round the beams, like images. There is room
for larger canvasses to be displayed, there are storing-places
for our weaker efforts; hold

to warm clothing, to surreptitious nips of spirits
hidden behind the instruments of art. It is all, ultimately,
a series of bleak self-portraits, of measured-out
reasons for living. Sketches

of heaven and hell. Self-portrait with computer;
self-portrait, nude, with blanching flesh; self
as Lazarus, mid-summons, as Job, mid-scream.
There is outward

dignity, white shirt, black tie, a black hat
held before the crotch; within, the turmoil, and advanced
decay. Each work achieved and signed announcing itself
the last. The barn door slammed shut.

*

There was a pungency of remedies on the air, the house
hushed for weeks, attending. A constant focus
on the sick-room. When I went in, fingers reached for me,
like cray-fish bones; saliva

hung in the cave of the mouth like a web. Later,
with sheets and eiderdown spirited away, flowers stood
fragrant in a vase in the purged room. Still life. Leaving
a recurring sensation of dread, a greyness

like a dye, darkening the page; that *Dies Irae*, a slow
fret-saw wailing of black-vested priests. It was Ireland
subservient, relishing its purgatory. Books, indexed,
locked in glass cases. Night

I could hear the muted rhythms in the dance-hall; bicycles
slack against a gable-wall; bicycle-clips, minerals, the raffle;
words hesitant, ill-used, like groping. In me the dark bloom
of fascination, an instilled withdrawal.

*

He had a long earth-rake and he drew lines
like copy-book pages on which he could write
seeds, meaning – love; and can you love, be loved, and never
say 'love', never hear 'love'?

The uncollected apples underneath the trees
moved with legged things and a chocolate-coloured rust;
if you speak out flesh and heart's desire will the naming of it
canker it? She cut hydrangeas,

placed them in a pewter bowl (allowing herself at times
to cry) close by the tabernacle door; patience in pain
mirroring creation's order. The boy, suffering puberty, sensed
in his flesh a small revulsion, and held

*

hands against his crotch in fear. Paint the skin
a secret-linen white with a smart stubble of dirt. The first
fountain-pen, the paint-box, pristine tablets of Prussian Blue,
of Burnt Sienna – words

sounding in the soul like organ-music, Celeste and Diapason –
and that brush-tip, its animated bristles; he began at once
painting the dark night of grief, as if the squirrel's tail
could empty the ocean onto sand. Life-

drawing, with naked girl, half-light of inherited faith,
colour it in, and rhyme it, blue. In the long library, stooped
over the desks, we read cosmology, the reasoning
of Aquinas; we would hold

the knowledge of the whole world within us. The dawn
chorus : *laudetur Jesus Christus;* and the smothered,
smothering answer: *in aeternum. Amen.* Loneliness
hanging about our frames, like cassocks. New

*

world, new day. It is hard to shake off darkness, the black
habit. The sky at sunset – fire-red, opening its mouth
to scream; questions of adulthood, exploration of the belly-flesh
of a lover. It was like

the rubbling of revered buildings, the moulding of words
into new shapes. In the cramped cab of a truck she, first time, fleshed
across his knees; the kiss, two separate, not singular,
alive. It was death already, prowling

at the dark edge of the wood, fangs bared, saliva-white.
Sometimes you fear insanity, the bridge humming to your scream
(oil, casein, pastel) but there is nobody to hear, the streaming river
only, and the streaming sky; soon

on a dark night, the woman tearing dumbly at her hair while you
gaze uselessly onto ashes. Helpless again you fear
woman: saint and whore and hapless devotee. Paint your words
deep violet, pale yellow,

*

the fear, *Winter in Meath, Fugue, the Apotheosis of Desire.*
The terror is not to be able to write. Naked and virginal
she embraced the skeleton and was gone. What, now,
is the colour of *God is love*

when they draw the artificial grass over the hole, the rains
hold steady, and the diggers wait impatiently under trees? Too long
disturbing presences were shadowing the page, the bleak
ego-walls, like old galvanise

round the festering; that artificial mess collapsing
down on her, releasing a small, essential spirit, secular
bone-structure, the fingers reaching out of *need*, no longer *will.*
Visceral edge of ocean,

wading things, the agitated ooze, women on the jetty
watching out to sea; at last, I, too, could look
out into the world again. The woman, dressed in blue, broke
from the group on the jetty and came

*

purposefully towards us, I watched through stained glass of the door,
and loved her. Mine the religion of poetry, the poetry
of religion, the worthy Academicians unwilling to realise
we don't live off neglect. Is there

a way to understand the chaos of the human heart? our
slaughters, our carelessness, our unimaginable wars?
Without a God can we win some grace? Will our canvases,
their patterns and forms, their

rhymes and rhythms, supply a modicum of worth?
The old man dragged himself up the altar steps,
beginning the old rites; the thurible clashed against its chain;
we rose, dutifully, though they

have let us down again, holding their forts
against new hordes; I had hoped the canvas would be filled
with radiant colours, but the word God became a word
of scorn, easiest to ignore. We

*

came out again, our heartache unassuaged.
The high corral of the Academy, too, is loud with gossipers,
the ego-traffickers, nothing to be expected there. Self-
portrait, with grief

and darkening sky. Soon it will be the winter studio; a small
room, enclosed; you will sit, stilled, on a wooden chair, tweed
heavy about your frame, eyes focused inwards, where there is
no past, no future; you sit alone,

your papers in an ordered disarray; images stilled, like nests
emptied; the phone beside you will not ring; nor will the light
come on; everything depends on where your eyes
focus; when

the darkness comes, drawing its black
drape across the window, there will remain
the stillness of paint, words on the page, the laid down
instruments of your art.

THE STUDY

Over the deal table a flower-patterned oil-cloth;
the boy
has his Bible history open before him, its pictures

of deserts, and of stylised heroes of God's militias;
he is chewing on a pencil-end
as if hunger for knowledge frustrates him and he spits

small splinters out onto the stone-flagged floor;
outside
hydrangeas are in bloom, their sky-blue flowers

big as willow-pattern plates; on the kitchen wall
a picture of Jesus, stylised,
fingers long as tapers, ringlets honey-brown, and eyes

lifted querulously towards the ceiling;
a red, eternal light
flickers weakly below the picture;

but the saddened eyes have lowered, and peer
down on the restless
stooped-over boy, in anger or in mute and trenchant

pleading;
and only a summer bee
distraught against the window, makes any sound.

CARPENTER

Grandfather's grave
lies amongst rank disorder; a high stone cross
holds the history of the world
carved in pastel-coloured lichens; the graveyard path

hides in weeds and grasses; St Joseph lilies flaunt
white and unkempt surplices; it is creation's
original chaos of delight —
where the old man lies, at peace, like God

before he shook himself out of lethargy
and spoke – *Let there be light…* But at times,
on quiet summer nights, the old man takes a turn
about the yard, tidying away

the empty beer and cider cans, the condoms,
and works a while on polishing his soul
against the final word that will draw
everything back to stillness – the way he used to hone

his workshop tools, because the old man's God
was a carpenter God
whose every word sent some new craftwork out
into the universe

to spin, and swell, and reproduce. You can hear
grandfather make his way back down,
sounds like wood shavings being swept,
like a workshop door being shut.

YOU

I am sea-born, and sea-inclined; islanded
on this earth, dragged each-which-way, and tidal;

senses shifting as the sands shift, my soul
flotsam. Prisoned in time, and you, love,

are eternity, you are the current in my depths,
my promised shore. And when I part from you,

taking my words to dry, sophisticated places, I am
tugged towards you, sweet desperation, this underwater storm.

CARNIVAL OF THE ANIMALS

Someone played piano in a far room: scales
growing out of black earth, blossoming, and falling back.

*

From outside, a cock's
hilarious response, all his hens
busily indifferent to his brass ego, indifferent too
to the honed axe-blade, waiting in the dark outhouse.

*

Badger, noon-time, after his night
hours of raids and rhapsodies,
roadside lies in dust, the stench of his decay
ghosting already on leaf and mayflower.

*

Cat comes, secretly, to the lupin-beds
to dream, will leave
bruised warm spaces, cat-sweet, like dreams; and big
bucko the hare comes lolloping through the wild meadow
to chew on the salt new leaves of the rose-bush;

*

for a moment, attendant on what is beautiful, I forgot myself.
But someone called from a far room: *John! John!*
and I was back again, in sunlight, hearing pitched
ongoing vibration of the one word: God; with the discordant

*

note: man, the un-
merciful; and the old song we all sing: God
is. And we
are not.

TO BE AS ONE

Bring me ashore where you are
    that I may still be with you, and at rest.

Your name on my lips, with thankfulness,
    my name on yours, with love.

That I may live in light and know no terror of the dark;
    but that I live in light.

When I achieve quiet, when I am in attendance,
    be present to me, as I will be to you.

That I may hear you, like a lover, whisper *yes* —
    but that you whisper *yes*.

Be close to my life, my loves, as lost son to mother,
    as lost mother to son.
        But be close.

Come to me on days of heat with the cool breathing
    of white wine, on cold
        with the graced inebriation of red.
            But that you come.

That you hold me in a kindly hand
    but that you hold me.

Do not resent me when I fail
    and I fail, and I fail, and I fail.

That I may find the words.

That the words I find to name you
 may approach the condition of song.

That I may always love with the intensity of flowers
 but that I love,
  but that I always love.

THE RED GATE

Mornings, when you swing open the red gate –
admitting the world again with its creeds and wars –
the hinges sing their three sharp notes of protest;
you hear the poplars in their murmurings and sifflings
while the labouring high caravans of the rain
pass slowly by; it will seem as if the old
certainties of the moon and stars, mingled
with the turnings and returnings of your dreams, mist
to unreality, although there rise about you
matins and lauds of the meadow-sweet and rowan; the first
truck goes ruttling down the wet road and the raw
arguments, the self-betrayed economies of governments
assault you so you may miss the clear-souled drops
on the topmost bar that would whisper you peace.

THE CHAPLET

I can go back, quiet as a ghost, from here
where sweet coals whisper in the grate, I can go back –
while hailstones sputter against the panes outside – to see her
standing in the doorway, snow falling softly, an old-woman's
spotted apron holding her, and know that she
is watching too, ghosting inwards and going back, visiting
her losses, as if she could find a way
to string it all together, to a sentence, making
sense, and I can sit remembering –
and shaping, the way a sonnet shapes –
that dusk her rosary burst asunder and beads
spilled skittering all-which-ways on the stone floor
as if her prayers and aspirations left
nothing in her shaking hands but a thread, bereft.

SLIEVEMORE: THE ABANDONED VILLAGE

You park your car on a low slope
    under the graveyard wall. Always
there is a mound of fresh-turned earth, flowers
    in pottery vases. There is light, from the sea and the wide

western sky, the Atlantic's
    soft-shoe nonchalance, whistle
of kestrels from the lifting mists, furze-scents, ferns, shiverings –
    till suddenly you are aware

you have come from an inland drift of dailiness to this shock
    of island, the hugeness of its beauty
dismaying you again to consciousness. Here
    is the wind-swept, ravenous

mountainside of grief; this is the long tilted valley where famine
    came like an old and infamous flood
from the afflicting hand of God. Beyond all
    understanding. Inarticulate. And pleading.

Deserted. Of all but the wall-stones and grasses,
    humped field-rocks and lazy-beds; what was commerce and family
become passive and inert, space
    for the study of the metaphysics of humanness. You climb

grudgingly, aware of the gnawing hungers,
    how the light leans affably, the way an urchin once might have watched
from a doorway;
    you are no more than a dust-mote on the mountainside,

allowing God his spaces; you are
    watercress and sorrel, one with the praying of villagers,
one with their silence, your hands
    clenched in overcoat pockets, standing between one world

and another. It has been easier to kneel
    among the artefacts in the island graveyard, this harnessing of craft
to contain our griefs;
    here, among these wind-swept, ravenous acres

where we abandon our acceptably deceased to the mountain earth.
    In grace. In trustfulness.
This, too, the afflicting hand of God. Beyond all
    understanding. Inarticulate. Though in praise.

TOWARDS A CONVERSION

There is a soft drowse on the bog today;
the slight bog-cotton scarcely stirs; for now
this could be what there is of universe, the far-off
murmuring of ocean, the rarest traffic passing, barely

audible beyond the hill. I am all attention, held
like a butterfly in sunlight, achieve, a while,
an orchid quiet, the tiny shivering of petals, the mere
energy of being. Along the cuttings

bubbles lift through black water and escape, softly,
into sunlight; this complex knotting of roots has been
an origin, and nothing new nor startling
will happen here, save the growth of sphagnum

into peat; if this is prayer, then
I have prayed. I walk over millennia, the Irish
wolf and bear, the elk and other
miracles; everywhere bog-oak roots

and ling, forever in their gentle
torsion, with all this floor a living thing, held
in the world's care, indifferent. Over everything
voraciously, the crow, a monkish body hooded

in grey, crawks its blacksod, cleansing music;
lay your flesh down here you will become
carrion-compost, sustenance for the ravening roots;
where God is, has been, and will ever be.

HARBOUR: ACHILL ISLAND

The winds come rushing down the narrow sound
between islands; from the north the whole
ocean pours through, exploding against boulders,
against landfalls, and courses into quiet
when the tide brims. A seal
lifts its grey-wise head out of the current, a mackerel
shoal sets the surface sparkling as it
passes. After the storm, light across the harbour
is a denser grey, soft-tinged with green; the whip
suddenness of lightning has shone this stolid
stonework fragile for an instant and the downpour
is a chariot drawn by six roan horses
pounding in across the sea. To the eye the water's
stilled now in the bay; stones on the sea-bed
shimmer like opals, cantankerous crustaceans
side-legging across the sand. I stand
awed again that this could be the still
point of all creation, the fruits
of a crazy generosity, yet how we amble through it
as if it were our portion, and our endeavour.

THE POEM OF THE GOLDFINCH

Write, came the persistent whisperings, a poem
on the mendacities of war. So I found shade
under the humming eucalyptus, and sat,
patienting. Thistle-seeds blew about on a soft breeze,
a brown-gold butterfly was shivering on a fallen
ripe-flesh plum. Write your dream, said Love, of the total
abolition of war. Vivaldi, I wrote, the four
seasons. Silence, a while, save for the goldfinch
swittering in the higher branches, *sweet*, they sounded,
sweet-wit, wit-wit, wit-sweet. I breathed
scarcely, listening. Love bade me write but my hand
held over the paper; tell them you, I said,
they will not hear me. A goldfinch swooped,
sifting for seeds; I revelled in its colouring, such
scarlets and yellows, such tawny, a patterning
the creator himself must have envisioned, doodling
that gold-flash and Hopkins-feathered loveliness. Please
write, Love said, though less insistently. Spirit, I answered,
that moved out once on chaos... No, said Love,
and I said Michelangelo, Van Gogh... No, write
for them the poem of the goldfinch and the whole
earth singing, so I set myself down to the task.

KANE'S LANE

The substance of the being of Jesus
sifts through the substance of mine; I
am God, and son of God, and man. Times I feel

my very bones become so light I may
lift unnoticed above Woods's Wood and soar
in an ecstasy of being over Acres' Lake; times again

I am so dugged, so dragged, my flesh
falls granite while a fluid near congealed
settles on my heart. The Christ – frozen in flight

on the high-flung frame of his cross
leaves me raddled in the grossest of mercies
and I walk the length of Kane's Lane, on that ridge

of grass and cress and plantain
battening down the centre, I sex my tongue
on the flesh juices of blackberries, cinch my jaws on the chalk

bitterness of sloes, certain and unsettled,
lost and found in my body, sifted through a strait
and serpentine love-lane stretched between dawn and night.

THE MARBLE RAIL

I came up against the marble rail, carrying
a weight of Latin and other mysteries: men
on the left side, women on the right. I got down
to studying heads of horses on the women's scarves,
how big men knelt, one knee down on cap or hanky,
left hand to the jaw, eyes loose, fingers twitching.
There was acknowledged presence of a people's God,
snuffling, reticent, unwilling and cajoled.
I took the strange moon-bread they fed me
and turned a half a century down the aisle
to where I still attend, waiting among a frail
seniority of old Ireland, and the blood of the God
has the savour of vintage sherry and His flesh
is a thickening of ashes across the tongue.

ON THE EDGE

In retrospect
there was a tenderness to the day,
a delicacy in the midst of dread;

in the year's completion –
hydrangeas soggy brown, the plum tree branches
black and brittle – there were yet

clusters of snowdrops
as in the blest beginnings, while the wind
spirited signatures across the rancid grasses

and playfully
erased them. The winter day
stretched clean and bright, the coffin came to rest on spars

over the deep-dug grave
like a new ship waiting to be launched.
In retrospect

there was a homeliness to the field
in its cold purity, while a train went by
beyond the trees and a plane rose, shimmering,

into the bluest sky.
We were holding on to the last prayers,
to the better memories, to the harmonies of wreathe

and bouquet; I thought
of last night's waking, only his face
visible above the lace and silk, like a mild

Quixote or a Frans Hals
grand seigneur. Now we were
holding on, the gravediggers waiting patiently

nearby. Then
he was lowered, the willful rites
completed, we, with the brute and idling earthedness

standing numb, complicit
in the necessity of things. A flight of wood-doves
passed like an exhalation over our heads, the wings

applauding loudly;
and there was order everywhere. In retrospect
there was something beautiful to the day. And unacceptable.

i.m. Gerry O'Malley

STILL LIFE

The generations have been slipping by here
scarcely noticed; the trees we planted,

oak and birch and eucalyptus,
scarce reached our knees those days, now they rise

stooping amongst scattered stars, against
turquoise deepening to blue-pink, emerald, cobalt.

We know, after the old folks with their hearth-music
abandoned us, generations are layered beneath, and still

the young hare leaps in the joy of morningflush
while the mismatched mistlethrush will cock

her speckled chest into the northern breeze,
as it was, we say, in the beginning.

I will turn soon into the broth of dreams,
blue-pink, emerald, cobalt, a blade of grass

of being, but for now I hold my hand
against the sky and watch a star

between my fingers, see the webbed flesh, feel the blood
pulsing, and listen to the soft sigh lingering.

for Michael Schmidt

EYE OF THE HARE

There! amongst lean-to grasses and trailing vetch
catch her? – vagrant, free-range and alert;
I saw the eager watch-tower of the ears, I knew
the power of legs that would fling her into flight;

concentrate, he said, and focus: you must love
the soft-flesh shoulder-muscles where the bullet bites,
caress – and do not jerk – the trigger: be all-embracing, be
delicate. I had no difficulty with the saucepan lid

down at the end of the meadow, lifted, for practice,
against the rhododendron hedge, I could sight
its smug self-satisfaction and shoot a hole
pea-perfect and clean through. Attention to the hare

left me perplexed for I, too, relish the vision
I imaged in its round dark eye, of a green world
easy under sunlight, of sweet sorrel and sacred herbs –
and I turned away, embarrassed, and absolved.

CEDAR

In what year of war did Jehovah
abandon them? A man
riding a Yamaha XS 400 model 1982
has taken his two daughters from the ruins of their house,
has left the battered bodies of his wife and mother
among the rubble and tries to flee
across the baked, beloved fields of Lebanon –
into a hole somewhere, please God, the two
children, terrified, big eyes filled with tears, fingers
gripping hard but the bike will scarcely move, it sputters,
skids,
one child before him, one behind, both tied to him
with light-blue clothes-line round their waists, the bike
slithers out into the day and turns, please
God, north on a cratered road, the sky itself so beautiful, such
an immaculate creation, and the children's' voices wail
louder than the stop-go reluctant coughing of the bike
till an Israeli F16, inaudible, well-nigh invisible, so high
above, oh God please God, draws
a gash of fumes across the sky
and father, daughters, bike explode into shards
of flesh and chrome and are lost
in the bleak inheritance of the Old Testament
while only the back wheel of the bike
a Yamaha XS 400 model 1982
spins in uproarious speed and will
not stop, will not
stop

THE COLOURS

These the colours of the seasons: gold
for the portal flowering of birth; violet

for shy kisses in a shaded copse, for days
of fast and pleading, for the iris of Van Gogh;

rose, for one long day of joy, for the survival
of sea-thrift on a famished cliff-face ledge;

suburban avenues will be clothed
in the alb of cherry-blossom white;

white and gold the chasuble
of the chestnut tree, and white

for angels flying in to the festival of snow, for virgins
crossing all together the frozen ice-paths of the Alps;

red, for martyrs, for the late-year standing of the dogwood,
the gift of tongues, the long delay of Good Friday

and the blood-stained building-blocks of Gaza;
green, for the ordinary days, *de tempore* labouring,

for past-time, in-between times and times ahead of times;
gold again, for the mind's embossed

portal to the sacrament, and black
for the peaceful, the having-come-through, dead.

SHOEMAKER

He sat, cross-legged, on a deal table
as if dropped, ready-made, from an old myth;
sat, all hours, all days, lips pursed and fingers
deft and fast, like the poet

who could see the world through a needle's eye,
difficult though penetrable, a shifting, leathery mass
that might be shaped to something
beautiful, and lasting. Like the itinerant Christ

walking the ranges of Galilee, nowhere to lay down
his head. When I conjugate
Christ, and longing, what I mean
is the lake behind the cobbler's house, its waters

soothing us constantly across the night;
I mean trees, those summer mornings,
standing high and stilled within their being; on wilder days
the winds make shapes amongst them,

ghosts visiting the house, composing
their wind-leaf harmonies: I want to be able to say, again,
Christ. Our island shoemaker
sat, sometimes, outside, half-concentrating, half-

watching people go the road; he was one
in a guild with swallows and the blooming of the haw,
one with the people who went measuring their steps
in to the small chapel to divine their living, who watched

snow falling, visible through the stained-glass windows, flakes
that could be birds migrating, butterflies, or spirits
out on spirit escapades. When I write
cobbler, last or nail, or when I scribble

wine, or bread, or music, what I am stitching for
is Christ, is how love still may permeate
the rush of trucks along the motorways, spray
rising against the windscreens, the wipers sighing.

BIKES

At the crossroads a big, joint-squealing gate
lead from the back yard to the road, an opening
out from the known world. Neighbours came
to leave their high-framed dray-horse bikes
slouched to the wall inside the gate, and took the bus
to their destinations. We assumed free rein
and took to pedalling round the yard, the bikes
bucking like jittery donkeys at our hands. But oh
how we raced, wee riders, relishing all the while
a watchful guilt, a boldness always on the point
of tears at a gashed knee or a sideways fall
into a tangle of chain and handlebars. We earned
accumulated secrecies when the travellers returned
puzzled at fine-groomed bikes standing to attention.

MIDSUMMER POEM

These are the grey nights, high tide, high summer.
Ash-trees in the hedgerows are stirring in the mists
and you can see the fields laid out in shifting patterns;

somewhere in the night a cow is lowing, sorrowful
as a distant foghorn; dreams are disturbed, something
gleams a moment and will disappear, like a sea-trout

rising, like a distant phosphorescence; breezes
that come shuffling through the alders are the breathing
of waves against a strand; no need to fear

ghosts of your loved dead who go drifting by, offshore,
their dark sails holding; the Joseph lilies, the white
Canterbury bells, hold within them, as you do,

their own light and though they will sink through the rough
autumn days, as you will, they have worked wonders
and will resurface, firmer in themselves and more fruitful.

for Gerard Smyth

MIMIZAN PLAGE

I know the meaning of the words: *hosanna* and *halleluia*,
the shout, and the long-drawn-out quavering belly-note:

Betty, who would not dance, dancing for exuberance
on the scullery table and Gerry shouting *Dia leat!*

you, on the beach at Mimizan;

porpoises beyond the waves at Keel, in slow ballet
over and under the ocean, stitching the sea to sky;

and you, on the beach at Mimizan;

Róisín, not watching, Tim watching out
as the car climbed through mile-high Italian villages;

you, on the beach at Mimizan;

jasmine blossoms, like milk-stars brilliant
against a dark-green sky, scenting the suburbs;

and you, on the beach at Mimizan, the red wine warming,
salamis, olives, rolls, and our hearts thundering.

MORE

There is more to it than the whimsy
of body or of mind. More than the quiet

of a pitch-skin currach upside-down on stones
where wind and windlass and hawser

rust-meld one to other at the pier's end.
It approaches the heaving of the sea, even, at times

the crashing of waves against the coast
in dark-day Atlantic storms. More than the lilt

of a Brandenburg concerto, or the shudder comes
at the perfect conjunctions of language. Near to prayer

but passing beyond. A reminiscence. A profound
expectancy. Something so great it judders

always beyond reach, the way the ocean shifts
in darkness past the strand-lights of the bay,

past the mast-bells and the wine. More than the waters
of all the oceans. The all of it. Then more.

for Ursula

SNOW FALLING ON CHESTNUT HILL

Traveller

'One day when we were young
One beautiful morning in May…'

A pair of mallard
circled down out of a dark sky
and skidded-splashed onto the surface of the lake;
peat-brown feathers of the she, her oboe-call,
the iridescent emerald of the he, his self-importance;

in the top corner of the wild meadow
suddenly foxes: sun on the red-gold pelts,
vixen-play wary with the fox-cubs' swift
tumble and paw-swipe on the grass, small
piccolo-skreeks and high-barks;

from the house the sound of the old Dansette,
a wobbling record, (His Master's Voice),
and Tauber's off-white tenor, the reedy
nasal crooning: 'Roses are shining in Picardy'.
I had been watching father, the beloved

– turned suddenly hunter –
lift down the sleek and hard-shod rifle,
select a blunt-head gold-red cartridge and slick it
into the breach; I knew the bullet-crack would shatter
fur and flesh and bone and end the music.

*

When I first saw the travellers
they were halted in the shadow of a hill, there
as if birthed out of night;

a caravan, green-drab, with a tarped
dirt-black tent drawn in
under the lifted shafts of a cart;

mute and rangey dogs
scavenged the borders of the camp,
a horse and mule –

crestfallen and watching towards unfathomable places –
stood braced against the day; children stood
in ragged smocks, finger-in-mouth and big-eye watchful;

there were stones
set to the wheels of the caravan, for keeping,
lest it off suddenly, and bolt.

When I passed home from school, a thick
unsatisfactory smoke was rising;
the children rooted with the dogs

in the measling chaos of pots and scattered blankets.
At home the adults
prated of violence; they told of stolen

hens and eggs, clothing missing off the lines, told
of night-time forays, bodies slipping through the dark
and making the darkness bleed. Once

the big man, dark-clothed, dark-fleshed, came
obsequious, cajoling, to our back door;
Tauber was singing, from the drawing-room

When they begin the beguine,
it brings back a night of tropical splendour...

the big man
eyed me, and I knew a small,
inexpressible, guilt.

*

I had my own immaculate days of lake and sky
and far-scented bog-sprung hillsides; I had
a crafted tub, rake for mast and sheet for sail;
to bump its prow against the black turf bank

in the sweetest influence of breeze
was all of adventure I then required;
I registered the fox-bark, how it told
a story of fugitive survival, I had found –

where the shore was dangerous
in reed-isle and moss-lawn – a trodden place,
an atrium before a dark lair, and a story-book
of hen-feathers, gristle-spit, and bone-claw. Once

*

I saw him, big-man, traveller, there
along my landing-place against the lake,
he was stooped over, and doing something;
I was scared of his gruff consonants, his black eyes;
I watched, as fox might watch from the archway of his lair,

and when he left I found
shore-stones darkened from a fire, burnt-black sticks
and up against the bank a midden
of eel-heads, eyes open in slime-black skin,
teeth bared and pin-sharp; the water,

amber-beautiful by the shore, became
a slaughter-place where long black eels emerged
from the peat bottom like filaments of mud, whiplash-fast
and slitherful and I heard, in dreams, the laughter
of the travelling man, and his camp's hubbub.

*

Muted trumpets, harp, the quivering strings:
Lonely on a desert breeze, I may wander where I please,
yet I keep on longing, just to rest a while.

They left, the travellers, as if a mist-filled daylight
swallowed them; there were small and ash-grey patches
clumped across the hill, with rags and timbers

and fox-red flitches of things along the thorns;
there were ash-smells and cooked-flesh fat-spills,
grease-puddles, a fungus-stink of oozed mud;

and I found it difficult to hold my place again
in the uneasy light they had left behind, a dusk-light
that kept on glimmering along once-familiar lanes :

MOTHER AND CHILD

Symphony of Sorrowful Songs: (Henryk Górecki)

You, God's flowers, lily white,
blossom on, you flowers of May
that my son, my beloved,
might sleep on peacefully.

Father spoke of Poland, of the girl who wrote
prayers on the wall of a cell
while the war of wars
went unabated. In December 1943 there were men

in Europe, falling on the soiled-snow battlegrounds,
flailing their arms
as if they would fashion out
snow-angels, who were jerking into stillness while the snow

covered them, only their hands lifting, their fingers
pointing. In a hospital, in the easy west,
a man stooped over a wicker-cot
and gathered in his arms the white body

of his new-born son. Sometimes I can share his wonder
as one small hand
closes about his finger,
my eyes shut, my being still shaking from the sweetness

of womb-cream, the rolling of the ever-shifting tides
of the eternal, my other hand
a fist, readying myself
for the battle, angered at my sudden, irretrievable loss.

*

One can say, in music, what cannot be said
when the forces of political oppression
are scourges through the fields and streets; there is
Palestine, and Syria, Ukraine... and then there is
Poland, the Warsaw Philharmonic, the slow
ponderous movements of the sacred spirit,
double bass to cello to viola to mother's voice,
sorrowful songs achieving passionate calm:

Mamo, nie płacz, nie.	Mother, don't weep, don't.
Niebios Przeczysta Królowo,	Most holy Queen of Heaven
Ty zawsze wspieraj mnie.	Help me now and always.
Zdrowaś Mario	Ave Maria

*

Dear, dead, Father:
                    I have put Górecki's 3rd Symphony
in the player; *sostenuto tranquilo ma cantabile*;
I see the mother's arms folded round her Son,
she rocks, slowly, over, back, in, out, the grief

rampant in the basses, this hopeless circling, mothers
against crucifixion: *Son, chosen and beloved one,*
let your mother share your wounds... I feel
despair oppressing me, the beauty of the songs

uplifting. When will we ever...? Will humankind...?
Mornings (do you remember?) opening
in delirious expectation the old stable door,
this day's light slanting in across last night's crop

of the whitest baby-tops, lifting themselves off the hot
and fragrant compost, reeking of horse.
In the darkened shed they spread themselves along,
a sanctity, graced by husbandry and night. Picked,

they came from the root with a hurt squeak and were ranged
in perfect order in the baskets, that precious whiteness
only the black of night can prosper, that hard-soft skin
resistant but nicked too easily to expose

the light-gold ribs; Pray, they urged in their regulated rows,
for us sinners, now and at the hour... like white
coffins of the children, Omagh, Srebrenica and Iran,
Angola, Kosovo, Israeli murdering in the Lebanon...

*

The red spot on the kitchen wireless
flickered;
there were whistling sounds, disturbances, they said,
from winds that blow
everywhere across the face of earth;

grandfather
leaned close, one big hand cupped to one big ear;
a polished voice came quavering
and fell away, flowed back, something about
the Korean war, atrocities, advances, the mounting

numbers of the slain; nothing new, the old man said, and spat
expertly on the fire.
Outside
trees were scuffling in an ever-present sea-shore dissonance;
I pressed my face to the window,

water-dribbles on the pane, and all the world beyond
was worried into breaking
patterns.
I crept upstairs again, to the bulked
and brass-hasped trunk; beneath the folded, moth-balled

oldsheets and lace cloths of Nanna's keeping, I found
the jacket of his uniform, peaked cap
with harp
and crown insignia and I marched
down-up, down-up, an RIC cadet, imagined pistols

manly on my hip. When I came down
grandfather was watching the labouring of the flames,
moist sods shifting as they burned; with a sigh
he settled back
and touched the dark-brown splotches on his wrist.

*

> *Ah, you wicked, wicked men*
> *in the name of God most holy*
> *why, oh why, have you killed*
> *my son?*

*

Dear Emily Maria,
We have learned how to bring the sky down, we are expert
at altering the weather and flinging our debris
against the face of Mars –

and we reached, in our time, zero point at 9/11
and where were we to go from there? down
minus? or take the first impossible step

towards the abolition of all wars?
The lamentation reads: *Because, dear son,*
I have carried you ever closer to my heart

and served you ever faithfully, speak
now to your mother, give her happiness, though already
you are leaving me, you, my hope, my cherished hope;

Emily, it goes on, from within the human heart...

Now you are four months old, and lie
peaceful in your mother's arms; Emily, there exists
unquestioning love, the wide-armed

all-embracing care of the Christ-man.

Alle Menschen werden Brüder   *All people will be brothers*
Wo Dein sanfter Flügel weilt   *Where your tender wing lingers :*

Snow Falling on Chestnut Hill
Denn alles Fleisch es ist wie Gras… (Brahms)

It is late now in the day; that curving lane
with grass and plantain, clovers and pimpernels
forming a hump along the centre, seems
to be straightening towards a conclusion. I have arrived

in a strange city, evening; (I am hearing
Brahms, the German Requiem, *Selig sind*…blessed
are they who mourn.)
Boston. A big house, and daunting.

They have warned me of arctic chill
reaching this way, over Canada, the lakes, Chicago;
Herr, lehre doch mich… I have heard already
oboe-moans through the eldering house, thin

reed-sounds through unseen interstices: O Lord
make me aware of my last end.
The hollow spaces of the house
are stirred along their dust: All flesh, the music tells,

is grass. I listened, dozing gently, silence
encompassing, engaging me;
at the front door I heard…
(no matter, it is no matter). I stood

watching first snow-flakes
visible against the street-lamps; there was the feel
as of the breathing on my face of a lover, as of the brush
of a kiss, sheer

arctic salt, a hosting. *Wir haben hier*
keine bleibende Statt...
All flesh
is snow. And snow

does not abide. *Selig sind die Toten*, blessed
are the dead; they are at rest
in the Lord's hands. I slept
fitfully; strange

land, strange house, strange dreams; time
raddling me. I could hear
the sound of the deepest night
lying still under a delicate coming down of snow.

*

I have been wondering
about our blizzards of pain and agony – Lupus, for instance,
immune systems down and civil war along the blood.
Prance of the alpha wolf. Bone

scaffolding showing through.
I lay, restless; my temporary home
whispered to itself in house-language, its wooden shifts
of consonants, its groaning vowels, when there came (Christ!)

a sudden rapping
against the door. I listened. Again,
rapping, urgent. I crept down. Opened,
I had to, street door, screen-door. Saw

darkness active out there, snow
swirling, a shape that
formed and faded out of the skirl of white and grey...
And she came, breathless,

shaking snow from her hair and face, stomping her feet,
stood in the non-light of the hallway and snow
pooled about her shoes. She, dressed in white,
reached to drop – 'a gift,' she said – one

bright Christmas rose, helleborus,
white-petalled, dark-green-leaved,
across the hallstand.
'You!' I whispered. 'You?'

She smiled.
'But we laid you down decades ago,' I said, 'to rest.'
'Isn't it good,' she said,
'to hear the crunch, under your feet, of fresh snow?'

'You are... in body, then?' 'Soul
and body, body and soul. No longer flawed.
I passed where snow is a swarm of whitest butterflies
though I had been growing old with the wolves.'

'And why? Why now? And how...?'
'I bring,' she answered, 'gifts. Wolves, too, wolves'
she whispered, 'wolves are the lambs of God.'
'Our child,' I tried, 'is wrapped up tight in pain, God's ways...'

(I saw, then, the wolf-pack, *canis lupus*, settling under trees,
they lie easy in the snow, you can hear their howl-songs,
clarinet-calls off-key in the moon-enlightened night, drawn-
out off-melodies, lauds chanted to the blood, their green-lit

white-shaded eyes sweeping across the heavens; *canis lupus*,
grey-grizzled ancients of days, the black, the white, the gor-
geous fur and in the distance I heard the freight-train howl
of human hungers, a tailed-off threatening horn-call across
the night; wolf-pelt, winter-pelt, the scars, the tissues, and
always snow falling down the everyvein of air)

'Be peacefilled now,' she said, softly as a brushing-by of snow,
'it is late, my traveller, live at peace in the rush
of arctic wind. We are all
sunlight, dimmed, all snowfall, thawed.'

'Our child...'
But she was already moving towards the door, her head
shaking; 'All flesh is snow,
snow-fox, snow-pelt I have been, with you,

a lover, singing against the moon,
a lamb...' The door... I felt the touch of pre-dawn frost,
heard snow in its soft slide, its fistfuls from the trees,
'Wolves, too,' she said, 'wolves

are the lambs of God'.
'Wait!' I called, and reached
for her. But she was gone,
suddenly, and there was nothing, 'I have

questions... prayers...'
Silence, only, and absence. I heard still
the breathing of the snow, a car somewhere
climbing a hill. I stood in darkness. Stood. Perplexed,

as always. A snow-plough passed, the steel blades
scraping against the roads. Soon
cars, roof-racked with snow, would shift
like herds of caribou

down the long parkway. The first
faint light of a new day
touched the window. I saw,
on the hallstand, fresh and beautiful,

one hellebore, one Christmas rose.
I closed my eyes against the dawn and heard
Brahms again: *Wie lieblich sind die Wohnungen...*
how beautiful your dwellings, Lord, how beautiful :

SEMIBREVE

I sat, in the island chapel, moor's edge, winter;
winds groaned and chistled round the walls outside,
the timbers creaked in the afterwarmth,

ghosts from the quenching slipped up through the rafters;
there was a souring emptiness though I sat entranced
by sacrament and my own minuscule being – when the walls

whispered – *Listen!* There was no-one. There was nothing.
Even the winds had died. And the chill winterlight
had dimmed. But a tiny chime had happened, vibrated

on my inner listening. The tiniest hint of spittle
tipped against my brow but there was nothing when I wiped
my hand across it. The door moaned again, a sudden breeze

forcing it and I stood, watchful, and shaken. That
was the first semibreve sounded of a gifted music.
I am day and night now, listening. Tuned for it, and waiting.

VIOLA D'AMORE

I had been playing Bach on the great organ –
'A mighty fortress is our God' –
the church below me empty in the nowhere afternoon,
bombarde, clarion, celeste

and when I lifted fingers from the keys
it was, for a moment, eternity, and the walls of the world
contained nothing but the lingering breadth of the harmony,

rafters of the loft had lifted while the whole sky
trembled in a breeze that rippled slow across it
till all I knew was the touch of the fingers of Jesus

soft on my fingertips, my body
consciously drawing breath, my bones
refusing their earthy weight, and my soul
ringing with immortality.

PLAYING ON THE WHITE NOTES

For days now, white butterflies are a storm
low over the meadow; they come to rest awhile
on the white clover, their wings, for a moment, folded;

the early purity of the lambs is a little sullied
while over against the fence line, Michaelmas daisies
are gathering to themselves the light of the sun,

hoarding the white heat of summer to their roots
as if the autumn colourings, waiting in the wings,
might be absorbed into the slow white dirge

the winter plays, when the black of night
will take its loveliness only from the white
splintering of stars, white fullness of the moon.

GREAT NORTHERN DIVER

Sometimes the sea, surging
through its seasonal gradations, comes

crashing in across the rocks and pier beyond Rusheen;
on Croaghaun the corrie brims,

dark water spilling over, gathering
a rust-brown iron and coursing down to ocean.

She who stands, this day, near dawn
to watch the morning bus out of Dooagh

leave for fresh-turned fields, stares vacantly out
over Atlantic waves that flick, sometimes, a salt spittle

against her face. She heard, last night,
the great northern diver far out, in the dark, offshore,

its long and withering cries, and she knows –
after the head-light beams of the emigrant bus

have passed on over the road and up the hill –
the rooster (cockerel, chanticleer, and cock-a-doodle-doo)

will be there, hoop-la, on the graveyard wall, crowing
his name out in a flustering of wattles, earlobes, crest.

Soon she will turn, to go indoors, wondering
if ever there is a time we are other than alone.

BLUEBERRIES
to Ursula

I am in California. The moon –
colour of grandmother's Irish butter – is lifting
over the Mount Diablo hills and the sky
is tinged a ripening strawberry. You sleep

thousands of miles from me and I pray your dreams
are a tranquil sea. Eight hours back
you watched this moon, our love-, our marriage-moon,
rise silently over our Dublin suburb, and you

phoned to tell me of it. I sit in stillness
though I am called where death is by; I am tasting
night and grief in the sweet-bitter flesh
of blueberries, coating tongue and lips with juice

that this my kiss across unconscionable distances
touch to your lips with the fullness of our loving.

EGG-WOMAN

She was widowed, young; three sons,
leaving her, gradually: for Coventry, Glasgow, Liverpool. She lived

tending graves; beating away
importunate ghosts. Sitting alone she whimpered sometimes,

like a favoured animal
kept outside in the rains. It was a long life, unaltering; perhaps

altering in the dark within.
Mouse-eared chickweed in the interstices of the shed, ebullient

rosebay willowherb
in the graveyard. She knew the every-morning miracle

of brown eggs stamped
with a small bronze feather, the every-evening watchfulness

of the vixen, of the slattern harrier hovering
over the scattered fluff-balls of fattening chicks. To be mother,

alone again, to sit by a chivvying fire
under the fading reproduction of Mary-in-Blue who held close

her golden son. She walked
the curious moist corridors between the graves, listening out for

greetings from her gravid neighbours
who used to walk with her on fair days and bonfire nights

to a celebration of the gift of flames.
Now she was nursing silence to her breasts, its threat, its intimacy.

NOVEMBER

Again the parlour has filled to overflowing
with the beloved dead – and I
stand distraught outside the great blurred window
looking in; little light where I am,

a soft persistent starlight; where they are, there are chandeliers,
though the dead are distant, a little
indistinct; they have been blown, perhaps, through the open door
into the hallway, like those several

beautifully-veined and parti-coloured leaves, old gold and scarlet,
from the trees that stand
bereft of summer, bare-head to the chilled and chilling
sky; and have wandered in

through that other door we never opened, and though they are
a little ruffled at the edges, a little
sere, they are upright and lightly swaying, the best crystal
in their hands; grandfather, possibly,

in the far corner, by the walnut cabinet, a vague
moustachioed figure, Nanna, wearing
her best of smiles, serving; closer, by the oil-lamp,
motherfather, fathermother, relishing –

as they never did before – a happy foolishness; closer still,
behind the net-curtained window, my
brother, cured of all ills, and laughing; there is a shadowy
and shrouded host-like figure

moving quietly amongst them, greeting them all with a little
banter. Ah well, we have allowed them
this one month to be amongst us, this first mustering
of winter, as if they were not always there

before our consciousness, calling out against our grieving.

NIGHT PRAYER
Rembrandt: Landscape with the Rest on the Flight into Egypt

I

This, too, you see, is prayer, these words I labour to admit
    under the spirit's prompting, words on the notebook
    difficult to decipher, the ink flowing out too fast

in the first stirrings; pen, copybook and keyboard
    in an attempt to touch the source of light,
    of life, the groundwork of our hope. Here, too,

II

figures in a nightscape, a pause in the difficult journey; questions
    of resting in penumbra, of knowing light is fragile,
    like a child holding its greedy mouth to the breast;

there is a fire of sticks, trouvaille of twig and branch, to keep
    wolves at bay, (between here and destination, Emmaus, say,
    beyond a life's full circle, light against the darkness) and this

III

is Jesus, name and nature of our source and sustenance, this
    is God, dwarfed by trees and distances, enormous landscape
    and a darkening night, and you grow aware that here the

watchful small lamps of greed and power are looming over all.
    The canvas, too, is prayer, impasto, brush and palette knife,
    working to ease the blackness about the light, cognisant

IV

of the death of innocents; it is all self-portrait, still life, a halt
    in the hastening, the helplessness of humankind before its own,
    the helplessness of God trusting Himself to flesh;

love is a small child, far from consciousness, hunted; should he be
    found and killed, what then? what then? Rembrandt
    knew that distance between himself and God – all time, all space, all

V

life, all death – had been too great; the instruments of art, sharpened and
    softened in the desiring heart, shorten the distance, finding
    a sheltering tree, light shouldering the darkness; this

Egypt of the imagination, this den of safety called
    exile, as world with its instruments of power and economics
    preys on you and how can you believe your pigments

VI

touch beyond impossibility? Image, less real than
    thistledown in a western gale, less permanent than golden light
    reflected on a pond, you try to empty the ocean of silence

with the holding power of pigments, the silence that is God.
    Christ-beyond-all-grasping, the heart in its pleading is a series
    of shifting darkscapes, vaulted in night-prayer passageways.

THE SWALLOW

You grow – like flowers from their soil –
   from the name and notion of your heart-place:
   Bunnacurry, Achill, Mayo; you are listening

– at the fleshly distance – to the music
   of the teeming hours, the prophecies;
   you dissipate, though slowly, what has been your essence

until you turn again, prodigal after years, on your journey
   back towards truth: the escallonia hedge, the baby-wail
   of the out-of-the-vertical back gate,

and to father, decades dead, watching. Now you stand
   at the harvesting of what has been
   the wild acres, terrified at the suddenness

of the years' passing, your quick tock-tick
   out of uncountable millennia, here at this damp meadow-edge
   to marvel at the swallow that has swooped across you

low over the meadow, that flash
   of red-rust feathers on the throat, and it is gone
   in a fling of its wings off up beyond the ash-tree hedge;

you write it down, then, in wonder, in words
   that are nets of air that cannot hold
   the mystery. You are working now towards silence,

admitting the absence of your father though he is still
   present in phlox and oxeye daisy, how you are –
   in this one moment – clothed again in home, become

the breeze beneath the swallow's wings, become
the sky, the murdered insect, the swallow,
become the prophecy and become, almost, the music.

JOHN CLARE'S BEDLAM

What do they pack for you in that battered suitcase
as they leave you to the madhouse door? How do they say

'goodbye'? how turn away? And how do you
turn from them, from the finches, from the sloe-

blossoms and music of the rainclouds – how do you face
towards that scanting cell? How will the warm sun's rays

discover where you are, all this not in the scheme
of God's devising? Can you sing while you suffer the severe

processes they have planned for your purgation?
– bleedings, chemicals – to turn the runnels of your brain

to oozings? And all the while the unfazed robin
calls you to rake for her the good, black earth again,

the fox would lead you down his trodden path, through
fragrances of pine, the tough-branched undergrowth you know

out to the heather marches where you would hymn, apart,
God and made-things, Christ and abundance, because the heart

is a shire too great to be enclosed, and the sky above is chaste
and shiftful as divinity, life-giving as the dark blood of the Christ.

THE SUMMER OF 2010
for Ursula

I have considered, often, how it might be:
turning in again at the red gate, you
and I, no more aged than we were then but just
as passionate, when it was April in the world,

when our carrier-bags of grief were empty
as they were when we first touched, that night
under the streetlamp in the smalltown square.
I have considered, too, how I would want to be

so still the kestrel knows me as rock or bush
as he hangs like the searing eye of God
over the heartland, I want to think that all of flesh
is cohort and endearing as the magenta beads

of our fragrant heathers. The Canterbury bells
you planted, the digitalis, the geraniums
are spreading their living colours before our window;
our dead, who have held their sorrowing

steadily against us, have moved on into their own
ideal orchards and we stand now, at peace together,
watching in awed astonishment how the eucalyptus
that we set down stands high in guardianship,

how a young child's voice calls out with joy
discovering orchids in the wild meadow: I see it all
as a music, rich as the great ninth symphony, the rhythms
inexorable, the key D minor, the harmonies assured.

THE SHOWER

And wasn't it something, after all, to be caught like that,
out in the world without coat or mac or brolly, foolish
in this our country? And taking refuge in a stand of trees,
rain plushing through the leaves and branches over you

and coming down in slow and generous drops and plops
missing you some of the time, sometimes not, and the sound
like a roomful of silent readers turning their pages all
together, till you felt embraced in your smallness

by the fragrance of rain over leaf-mould, by the green
darkness that held you, and the world out there so all
riven with grandeur and greyness that the drip drip drip

on your unprotected shoulder was the tap tap tap of someone
reminding you, just that, lest you forget, lest you take it
for granted: so you are glad you were unreasonable, unprepared.

THE STUMP

For many years the humming eucalyptus
offered abiding-places amongst its branches

in a warm and wind-wild festivity of foliage;
now, after prolonged snowfalls, after the murdering

frosts of winter, it is standing, dead. Scentless. Sounds
like dry skins rubbing against each other. The leaves

vanished, though in spring and everywhere around
trees and bushes reach again in baby-green,

vociferous in branch and foliage, and playful
in the breeze. The eucalyptus, not being family,

succumbed to this winter's persistent sorrowing.
Its bark has cracked, patchy in brown, it shrivels

and peels off, like an old man's wrinkled skin;
and I am remembering how the stars

played hide-and-seek amongst its leaves, how sometimes
the moon was lodged in its nets of branches.

What I am afraid of now is that the eucalyptus –
after it is felled and its dried-out bones have been

tossed into our stoves and fireplaces – will forget us,
forget how it sheltered, how it fed our several senses

and that all that will be left to us is a stump,
bland and featureless, like a once-familiar name.

THE PRIDE OF LIFE
for Tim Sheehan

McGarvey and I were young and male and speaking
of the concupiscence of eyes, of flesh,
of the pride of life; our God, old Taskmaster,
demanded of us perfection, suffering and Latin.

McGarvey and I were dressing boards
of flesh-coloured deal, dovetailing them
into library shelves when the chisel,
curved like the quarter moon, slipped, and sliced

into my index finger; maladroit, I watched
blood spurt until the pain scalded me
and I sat down, stunned, amongst wood-shavings
and white dust; *in illo tempore* seminarians,

McGarvey and I (like Christ himself) were in otherwhere
on carpentry assignment, though I was more
for the study of Aquinas and the Four Last Things, more
apt with pen and paper and the ancient texts;

my finger-flesh had lifted and I tied it, tight,
with my seminarian's white handkerchief – *you're
pale as a ghost*, McGarvey said, that ghost
still with me now, pen in hand, wandering the world,

a fine-curved scar on my index finger;
a solitary gladiolus, elegant and tall,
of a cardinal brightness, beckons to me
from outside the window, and that young seminarian –

misfit and eager, trenchant and melancholy
in the pursuit of love – haunts me still, his God
and McGarvey's God, displaced, replaced, my God
untonsured now, and feminine, and here.

A BIRTH

Yeshua, at your birth, did the angels
sing Vivaldi's *Gloria*? and the shepherds,
did they play jaws harp, Jews' harp, tonguing
Dvořák's *New World Symphony*? The spheres —
were they humming, as twilight turned
from tangerine to emerald, and down
to a drear and turquoise basso — did the stars
sound out Bruckner, Brahms and Bach?
That sheep may safely graze... Or was it merely
the snuffling of animals in their stalls, dawn-music
played each morning in the small farms, the opening
of stable doors, or city-sounds of preparation
for another day, like an orchestra tuning up, this
puer natus, this image of love, of God invisible.

MUIR WOODS, CALIFORNIA
October 22, 2010

Redwoods, sequoia sempervirens, steeple-tall,
where we walked, awed to silence, through a past
present to us in the trees, centuries old,
the soft rain's sibilance holding all the woods
in an embrace of stillness; down the rich aisles
of pillared trees that soared, reaching high
as old God's leaning, we found ourselves
insignificant, temporal beings, taken by the impulse
to pray; till we saw the owl, squat on a branch,
watchful Methuselah, barred owl, old hinge-head,
swivel-face and rain-owl, bemused at us who mooched
by below, uncertain, turning to our cellphones
for assurance, our cars waiting in the carpark,
urgent for the forecourts, the switchbacks, the freeways;
you could hear them, the redwoods, in the mists
gossiping about the restlessness of humankind,
who, for the moment, struggle with our illnesses,
with the loveliness of the roe-deer skittering
across our path, elegant and fearful, and the buck
quick in his balletic leap into the ferns till we know
we have dipped our fingers in a sacred font
and emerge, fortified by sacrament, blessed again in spirit
for our ongoing struggle with the flesh.

BUNNACURRY PIER
i.m. Declan Deane 1942-2010

It was morning then in the world, and we –
acolytes together – sang to the God who gave joy
to our youth. It is morning yet, in the still
backward of the soul that is memory, holding firm

across rise and ebb of happiness and grief. We ran
down to the pier, with makeshift rods, makeshift
lines and hooks, the waters of Blacksod Bay
brimming; we would be fishermen, we would be

fabulous, for the juvenile pollack came, *bullagógs*,
plumped to a silvering dark-green shape, big
as our father's thumb, flickering in the dark-green
tide; we caught them, baiting hooks with the drawn-out

flesh of periwinkles, hoisting the tiddlers proudly up
to the rough-stone pier. We were raucous together then,
content – for now – in the slow upwelling of our lives
and beyond us, out there, the continents, the tides,

the harbours. And now, after it all, the decades, the deaths,
does the heart still sing? Remember how the story-teller
asked: what are you afraid of? Don't you know that
once upon a time, Christ himself, our Little Father, died?

ENCOUNTER

It is March; in Ireland
daffodils will be suffering the harshest winds; here
the coach had turned back from the slopes of the Beatitudes
towards Tiberias; to the right

the valleys, green and flush,
rising to the hills; to the left, the lake, quietened
in an evening lull and pleasuring.
I settled in my seat, comforted, and tired; when –

and this is my wakeful dream, the happening, the real –
in the coach-seats opposite, father,
fisherman and March-month birthday-boy,
and brother, Declan,

impatient God-lover, picketer by the gates
of San Quentin, celebrant of falling free at last
from alcohol addiction: both of them
in animated conversation, both of them dead

for years, and months; they spoke
in a language without words, song-like, seductive.
Outside, darkness was falling early, the sun
a dying fire, light catching

on the thorn of the moon that was lying idle
in a sapphire-shaded heaven; soon there would be shimmering
silver nightways out across the sea. Father
suddenly called to me, and pointed; the bus

stopped, and we stepped down, we three, only;
silently they walked across the grass, down
towards the shore;
drawn, confused, I followed,

the light so faint now all was shadow,
father, old friend, and faithful; Declan, brother, and priest.
The old man turned to me, and smiled, 'we', he said, 'we
are not in death, we are in life'.

He pointed. There was another
standing near the lake, her back to us, she was watching
out over the water, frail-boned, slight
but firm. 'Mother?' I said and she turned,

slowly; I did not know her; fair-skinned,
handsome but not beautiful. 'Your name?' I asked;
'Miryam', she said, 'Miryam of Magdil. And yours?'
'Yohanan', I answered, to my surprise. Around us

ruins only, excavations, stone-heaps, stumps – Magdil?
'It was here,' she said, 'he
stepped ashore from the fishing-boat;
and stood awhile, gazing towards the hills; I

was kneeling, there, by that great rock;
I was gutting fish, for salting; I worried for his feet,
naked against the sharp edges of the shells;
the others, fishermen, moved awkwardly,

hauling the boat ashore, uncertain of themselves;
and 'who are you?' I asked him
though I already knew the answer; he
is the way, he is the life, and his truth

will sear both soul and body. And he said, 'Miryam',
as if he knew me; 'if I give,' he said,
'word of myself, what can that be to you? Come,
and see.' And I left fish, and shore, lake and village

and followed him. He is invasion, hero, mystery,
he is the centre, he is forgiveness, light. And now I,' she said,
'am in death no longer, I am in life.' She smiled,
turning back towards the sea;

I glanced for father, brother, but they were
not there and when I turned again, she, too, had disappeared.
I shivered suddenly, alone, and cold; a black-backed gull,
perched on the great rock,

was stabbing down
at some small feathered thing.
Now it was night;
from the road Abram was calling out to me

and I came back, shaken, challenged, but at peace.

MOUNT HERMON

And then we moved aside a while, outside
pilgrimage, to sit at table on the lakeshore terraces,
four or five gathered together, a presence amongst us
greater than our individual presences. The sun

was going down behind the city of Tiberius,
touching the Galil with fluid colours, and snow-bound Hermon
shifting from softest pink to rose, into a shimmering
soft-toned emerald, then shading down to grey. Israeli

war-jets flew shuddering the air over the lake, high
aggressive pterodactyls utterly out of place. We said the name,
Yeshua, Yeshua, shared wine and breads and oil, spoke of him

in sacrament and sharing. Word. Entire. Yeshua calling us
by name. I spoke a psalm, language but no words, within me.
We are witnesses to wonders, and we have news to tell.

WALLS

I stand – a continent away
from the crumbled walls of Bunnacurry 2-room school –
now, at last, by the Western Wall,
leaning my hands against its massive stones, and seeking words;

'in Yerushalayim', the Spirit wrote, 'shall be my name forever';

to my left, black coat and pants,
white shirt and thick grey beard, kippah, prayer shawl, a man
sways back and forth in prayer –
hear, O Yisrael, The Lord our God, the Lord is one... Torah, psalms;

our little catechism asked: *does God*

know all things? The high partition
between the rooms squealed on its castors, folding open,
when Father Tiernan came
to test our souls; *God knows all things, even*

our most secret thoughts and actions. I relished then

the loveliness of the near-rhymes,
the old-fashioned *doth*-and-*dost* of the English, leaving
a softly-furred coating on the soul. I need to know
the rough texture of a wall you could break your life against; and so

I have come to take possession, of the songs, the psalms, the lamentations,

Ruth and Boaz, Jonah,
Daniel in the den of lions – for these are my stories, too,
the prophet Moshe stretching out his hand
over the sea, Yermiyahu's grief before the golden throne

of Babylon, with Markos, Mattityahu, Loukas, Yohanan…

for here is the gate of Heaven, folded open,
where we thrust our words towards the invisible, waiting for those
inaudible answers, where we thrust our prayers
into the crevices in the wall,

and speak aloud, look, here I am, oh Elohim, oh Yeshua, here I am.

CROCUS: A BRIEF HISTORY

The crocus opens out to something
more than crocus, becomes a brief history
of time, the ology of cosmos, as a poem is –

impacted yellow of gold-dust, shape
of a baby-thumb all-tentative, prelude to a new year;
breath of fire from the dark earth, from the closed heart;

the rose-coloured: flush of love,
signature of the overture: – these sudden, these small
preliminaries – polyphony of crocus – demi-semi-quavers

of what will be an oratorio
of hollyhock, lupin, sunflower,
under the gold-full baton of the light.

for Thomas Peter Leonard

AN ELEGY

Flora in the roadside ditch
are boasting the water-colour purple of a pride of bishops –
vetch, knapweed, clover and the rosebay willow herb;
and I would make a poem

the way old Bruckner caught a flight of pelicans in his
Ecce sacerdos magnus…
for eight-part choir, key magenta, though these times the spirit
slumps, mal tended in this limping country. Now

a blackcap, fast and furtive, comes to feast on the white berries
of the dogwood hedge; bullfinch,
secretive, subdued, flit in a shock of rose-petal black and white
across the alder thicket

and I am urged to praise, willing to have the poem
speak the improbable wonderful. Today
the poet Seamus Heaney said he was leaving us for a while,
visiting high mountain pastures,

and seeing things.
I have been walking, grieved, the Slievemore heathlands
and watching a sheep-dog,
low-crouched, eager, waiting for the sheepman's whistle;

furze blazed with a cool gold flame; the sheep
were marked with blobs of red and purple dye, cumbered
with dried-in mud; while out on the bay
the Crested Grebe moved, masterful, in brown Connemara tweed.

Goldfinch, this morning, were trapezing on the teasels,
redpoll, siskin, shrike touched on the hazel tree;
under the whitesilk innocence of its blossoms
the hawthorn's limbs are twisted in their growth.

I was sitting under the eucalyptus tree with the old books,
Amos, Osee, Ruth. A slow mist had been slinking in
across the alder leaves and I could see the rushes,
still as rust-haired soldiers, waiting. I know –

because I have not spoken – I have unclean lips
and the roof of my mouth is turf-grit dry.
Jasmine, trailing across a wall, droops in an early chill,
hangs limp and festering; when it sheens again

the scent will fill the dusk with sweetness the way honey swabs
the mouth. Like birds, I am eating the seeds of praise,
of light and growth and seasoning, coming again to relish
rainfall on a roof of galvanize and the silver

of sunshine following: epiphanies, offering a language
to moisten the tongue with words. Now I watched
a tree creeper, like a mouse, work itself
up the bark of the eucalyptus; its scimitar-bill drew out

the white-fat larvae: obedient, I said, to its nature
as the distant hills take mythic colours from the haze.
I rose and closed the pages, content to touch on marvels
and walk the earth with hurting, Genesis feet.

GOLDCREST

Of course they come back, the dead, because they are there,
just beyond our being, on the other side
of that nothingness we are scared of, because there is work to do,
on earth and in the heavens,

and because we haunt them. We hear the intricate
tock-tick-tock of the wound-tight
innards of creation: Laudate Dominum, Hagia Sophia, epistolary
symphonies of St Paul.

But our New God is not the Most High God :
he is Burning-bush and Whinny-hill and Furze-bloom; he is not
a gilt tabernacle bathed
in ethereal light – but goldcrest, flitting in the berberis

for a feast of insect while snow
flurries down through a wash of sunlight this out-of-season
Easter week. God
is not *not*, unchanging, unbegotten, ineffable, God is *is*. So I

– remembering days when the pink rose
rambled, and blackberries plashed purple kisses on my lips – find
contentment this side of nothingness, and being
ghosted by the presence of those I have loved, and lost.

THE CURRACH

That summer the heavens opened;
days you'd think
Noah come again, eels
squirming in the streets and brown-water streams

harrowing the tarmac edges; birds
skimmed over the grasses, swallow, house-martin, swift;
starling flocks,
gossip-mongering in branches of the ash

lifted suddenly as one, though fractured,
sentence.
The coming by the house
of yet another downpouring of rain

sounded at first like the titter-tattering
legs of rats
racing across the stretched-taut skins
of tympani.

When they hoisted down an old upright piano
off the pier's edge onto a curragh
and rowed carefully out across the sound towards the island,
the rains came harder,

blotting out the world;
the boat lurched sideways into the reaching arms of a wave; piano
leaned lazily over and sank and now –
under the rough-cast gurgling cacophonies, the gripe-words

of the flowing past of waters – you will hear
the busy-fingered currents
perform a suite
of intricate and burble-delicate water-music.

THE RUINED MEADOW

Something of the reassurance of the seasons in it,
a tractor
out in the meadow, mowing; evening, high-sky blue,

and then the big machine on through darkness,
headlights
sending fence-post shadows through the window;

they move across the kitchen wall,
unholy shapes
shivering in a queasy silence. By morning

bales of light-green grass litter the shorn field.
Pigeon on the chimney-pot
hoo hwhoo hooed his love-call of sustained distress

echoing where the smooth presenter of this day's deadly news
spoke his own hoo hwhoos
into electric air. Syria, he said, the children… and stuttered

into silence. And then – billions of years in its fostering,
perched now
on the sheep-wire fence – there he was, robin, *spideog*,

with that engaging look-you-in-the-eye cockrobin-ness,
small chubby masterpiece,
created out of air and the plucky verve of spirit, plaything

of a fierce universe, reassurance, too,
in that sharp eye,
taking ownership of the mist, feasting in the tractor ruts.

COAST

They were standing in the belly of the trawler,
big men in from the sea;
on the black-wet boards at their feet

boxes of fish, fat and slippery, their round eyes open,
dulled and bulging;
the men, in their orange wind-cheaters, their scaled and blooded

grey slaughtering-aprons, heisted the catch up
onto the quay
before the bulged eyes of the tourists, creatures,

out of their element, alien here, and cold
in biting air off the Atlantic.
But tonight, in the scents of onions and olive oil,

of pepper, tomatoes, lemons, warmly-lit rooms will be humming
to the savouring of blood-dark wine,
the taste of the charcoal skin of a black sole.

THE ANGEL

Two years the eucalyptus stood, dead
in its place, the death angel hesitant
to abandon it. I touched the bark, sorrow
a sap rising within me. The tree had been
inspiration, its yielding scent, its leaves
quivering, its arms housed for a swarm of bees,
crossroads for the snattering of goldfinch,
secret crannies for treecreepers, for flycatchers.
Its death was unspectacular, freezing where it stood
through a desperate winter. Held on, suffering
the indignities of despoliation. Skin shedding
in long, dun scabs, spoiling the lawn. Till I knew
the tree's love was an intensity I cherished
for all those years. Chainsaw, finally, against its skin
was a caress, guiding it to its fall – the slow
creak of its splitting, the splintering, like stained glass,
of its lesser branches, the dull thump of its trunk
against solid ground – all this a farewell, a plea
for forgiveness. The angel left with a sigh, the emptiness
that stood against the sky was a spirit lifted into air
and held close after the flesh's long dormition.

HUNGER

I heard the barking of a fox,
urgent in the bitter-amber glow of the urban night; predator
through the small, untidy gardens,
she has perfected a steady loping, an easy watchfulness;

the glad and sorry facts of human living
are discarded packaging the fox-tongue probes, fox-eye
watches for. At the street's end
the traffic lights move on from red to green to amber,

nobody at this hour to heed them, these silent calls
to caution, to take care, survive.
In the sudden light the window throws, vixen looks up
from her hungers and is not stirred, she knows

the sound a back-door-click makes, knows too, perhaps,
that womanman, in its warm den, has its own hungers to satisfy.

TOWNLAND

Bethlehem: the village, and the townland,
crowded and expectant
like a fair day in Bunnacurry; in our dark cowhouse
there were snuffling sounds

and the warm, rich reek of cattle.
Bethlehem: Joseph and Mary standing,
wide eyes fixed on one another,
the whimper of a boy-child in between; brown earth outside

was frumped and sodden
under the slow breathing of mist. A harsh half-moon
shivered on the frosted road
down to the Bunnacurry church, and we, children,

bundled ourselves tight
in winter coats, our breathing forming angel-shapes
on the biting air. It was just a birth; one
out of millions that had come before, of millions

that would come after; this one birth
neither a beginning, nor an ending; a turning-point
merely, though shading all that went before, all
after, tossing the rags and peelings of time into the uncertain

texture of eternity. Bethlehem: stars
above the caverned escarpment. Crib and candle-light
in Bunnacurry chapel, where we knelt
awed by festival, by the silence surrounding, by the animals.

PULSE

Catwalks of goldfinch on the branches, in a fashion-parade
of colours, of party-feather boas; now, in dusklight,
the breeze is snuffling in the high poplars

in that gentling hour you stand, before sleep,
under the moon-sliced-in-two, while above you, you surmise
the snow-feather wonder of swans, the heart-beat effort

of wings in flight; and higher still the steady process
of a satellite moving to the same heart-beat.
Light from a window far across the valley goes suddenly

out; you know that, further off, in the tumulus at Newgrange,
swallows fledge down deep in the throat of earth,
preparing – on the marvel of their wings – a summer solstice...

Nonetheless, in the fleshly heart, there is again
news of the massacred laid out on a concrete floor
in Syria, rose-petal stains on the walls, and you turn away

to bow, a moment, in the quietness of prayer, in the ragged
shadow of the eucalyptus, while the tender wall of darkness
behind your eyes is edged for a moment in blood-light.

LETTER FROM EAST ANGLIA
for Dr Rowan Williams

Dear Pilgrims,

The light is a late autumn light, there is a certainty
of frost; trees – ash and maple and eucalyptus –

stand in their pastel colourings, the smaller roads
are damp after last night's star-rife sharpness

and will not dry out in these short, slatternly days.
Chill winds off the North Sea, East Anglia, cut to the bones,

skin is ragged, like shredding sails. In Norwich, in Julian's
modest cell, nobody comes calling, dry leaves hustled

by the breeze outside make the softest sounds. Candles,
and coins dropped into the wall-safe, are a pleading

that every manner of thing, on the journey, might be well.
In the market-square, a woman at her stall – herring

in from the North Sea – scrapes fish-scales and blood
from the boards with a killing-knife; Julian said –

Jesus is motherly, comforting in his homelyhood. We

have come on windy side-roads through the spreading pastures
of the Giddings, pilgrims, moving like flocks of foam

blown upon the sea. Small red apples scent the air
and feed the shadowed ground below; silence

holds the greening gravestones in a gossipy
lean-together in the church yard, while at times

the doves make mess among the pews and kneelers;
schoolchildren from the parishes, kneeling against

Ferrar's table tomb, sketch the peaked bell-tower
of George Herbert's church.

Dear pilgrims:

En-route to Little Walsingham, step in a while
to the Slipper Chapel,
and say some words to the Saxon Lady
Richeldis de Faverches;

there has been a breakthrough here into the impossible;
Annunciation Window
is a 40-voice motet in blue, from the dark of night
to the whiter blue of Mary's robe;

even the moon – announcing its scimitar-shaped *yes* in white –
is filled with crêpe-de-chine of blue;
what more there is of white is the sceptre Joseph lily,
a dove's flight that sets the black on fire;

the startling, stalwart angel – who blows in from the west –
does not seem out of place, place
that is chapel, that has been poorhouse, cowshed, forge – now
locus for dreams

and barn for the dance of possibilities – for the raising of a chorus
against the crowding in of sorrows,
a shoreline for the launching of the imagination
into the blue beyond of hope.

Listen! the still-young girl in question hears her name
spoken out, with feeling,
in the strangest tongue, hears words announcing nothing on this earth
will ever be the same again.

Pilgrims:

In Ely, shop-window canopies crackle in the wind,
like distant gunfire from a battle out on the North Sea.

The nave, in this great Ship of the Fens, is a redwood
forest of all-Saints, all-Souls, holding the history

of our salvation: Oak of Mamré, Jesse Tree, and Calvary…
In the Lady Chapel, the angel's words of greeting: his *ave*, his

sé do bheatha, his *je vous salue*… were words that made as one
the raw earth of our scrublands and the heaven of our hopes;

in the intertestamental sunshine you can hear the Virgin's
high shout *Magnificat!* and the long, reiterated litanies, humankind's

polyphony of pleas and pleading. A field-hawk, evening,
soars in ease over trim and dusk-lit small-towns of the shire.

ACCORDING TO LYDIA

Cock-Crow

It was soon after dawn and he was out already,
raw and impatient, for we could hear his axe
splitting wood, the first dull dunts, then the quick
rupturing sound, its echo against the roosters' calls;
there was strength and such assurance in the sound
the village came to itself with a morning confidence;
the thousand-year-old olive stumps resisted stanchly,
but he would later polish the wood to a perfection
smooth to the thumb. By noon he'd pause, listening
to the laughter of young girls busying themselves
among the vines. Then, in the afternoon loafing-hours,
he would slip away to some hidden wilderness
alone, as if fruits of earth and toil were slight. A shadow
would darken the woman's face watching from the doorway :

Bedrock

Wilderness. We heard first about locusts and wild
honey; then, demons and beasts. Sheer absences, no
water. Shade. Comfort. The sun so fiery that the low hills
shimmer like a mirage. There are cool, sheltering places,
occupied. Easy to believe in demons, so little sound
there the mind hums. By day the burning, by night
the crackle of frost; thudding stillness of the heart, admitting
wisdom, dust-awareness; immured in desert nothingness
and the struggle with the mind. Opening to loneliness,
to the holiness of the unresponding; garnering strength
against the worst that noon can do, or the trailing moon;

dying to flesh-hungers, earning a certainty
that washed him through with tenderness, that raked
spirit and flesh to a sheer, uncompromising love :

The Binding

The lake's edge – generation after generation
depending, shallow at the shores, bronzewater, gold;
millennia of shells, patterned dull and gay, becoming grit –
profound, a harvest, what's left of innumerable deaths.
They have drawn the boats up onto the grass, and sit
examining the nets; the human heart, they know, is forged
out of such bindings, such husks, at the very lip
of wilderness. This day, out of a sky so bright
it chafes like silver, they hear the high-pitched cry
of a swooping sea-eagle ripping the air. The man –
in mulberry-coloured robe and leathern sandals – has passed
down along the margins towards the boats; at once
there is disturbance, a sharp kerfuffle at the lake's edge
and the brothers, without a backward glance, forsake the shore :

Kfar Nahum

Beyond the village, willows, scrub grass, small waves
frivolously fingering the shore; warm breeze under grey,
scarce shifting, clouds; the day lifeless, and everyday
ordinary; a fishing-boat drawn up onto stones,
no shore-birds visible; noon, as if the world had
paused, uncertain, waiting. In the crumbling synagogue
craftsmen and fishermen sat, bemused, the stranger
standing before them, reading, and expounding; as if he bore
quietness in his bones in spite of the earthed resonance

in his voice; the authority, the unaccountable wisdom
that had been concealed somewhere in the Torah scrolls,
the mourners, the merciful, the hungry. Puzzlement
among them, here and there a muttering anger. Words,
as ours, but new, and other. A man like us. Unlike. But like :

Disturbances

By sunset, in Kfar Nahum, he had drawn to himself
many of the broken, crazed and trodden-down,
the undesirables, the pariahs and the freaks;
the space between gate and lake was a market-field
of clamour, pleading, incredulity and tears. Soon
he was exhausted. A yellow moon
hoisted itself slowly above the village, and a crow,
lifting in dudgeon out of the roost, called a loud
craw! to the clouds. By now, we were unsure of it,
what had happened, for something difficult
was insinuating itself within the stepped-out limits
of our life, but we knew there would be consequences,
grave. It was owl-night, the bird calling out 'who? who?';
can what is broken be whole again, what's crooked straight :

The Flowering

That night we lit lamps everywhere, outside, within,
on grass and pathway, down to the shore; he sat on,
all light and shadow, his words gathering radiance
and darkness into their texture; we lived a while in an island
of being, apart, and unmanageable; and oh! the strangeness:
a cock crowing, bright-winged moths singeing themselves
against the flames; smoke from the oils sometimes

itched the eyes but we stayed, startled when he said: *your*
sins are forgiven! and no-one, there and then, doubted it –
we thought of our blessed YHWH; we thought of the stone
heads and torsos of gods in the city set on their shaky
pedestals, and the night swelled; as if the raw green stem
of the Pentateuch were about, latterly, to open into
a great red wound, like the high and blossoming amaryllis:

Demons

It takes a lifetime to cast demons out;
you struggle with them, you, demoniac, you, unclean,
they throw you down, you howl inside, you get
up again, you have to. Lest they destroy you. He
touched them, lepers, too, their sores, their bandages,
their dead eyes. He would take all burdens on himself.
Thirsted and hungered have we, for such as he, to enter
into the soul's holding. I have found, down in my heart,
there is a sphere so still, so silent and untouched
it is pure as the snow-topped summit of Hermon
glistening in the distance. He came, gathering them all to table,
the manic, the castaways, the hobbled (we thought him mad)
and there was laughter, and quiet and – I tell you this –
peace where never there was peace, nor laughter ever :

Table

I need to tell of this, I need to set it down –
how he brought them in with him, and how they grinned
at the shaken host; servants, with disdain, offered water
for their hands and feet but the stranger knelt and
helped them: the beggars, the bedraggled, and the whores;

they reclined on cushions at the rich man's table: who did not
eject them, offering lamb and artichokes and goat's cheese,
wine and pickled fish and pastries soused in honey; they
asked for barley bread and barley beer. The stranger broke
and dipped the bread and passed it to them, told them jokes
and stories of lost sheep and prodigals and wheat seeds scattered
against the wind. It was, the host adjured, a ghostly meal, touched him
with joy and bitterness, this kingdom rife with casualties –
but it was I, he said, who found I was immured in poverty :

Samaria

Jacob's well, Shechem, route of nomads, revolt, crusade…
of people toiling down valleys of silence into exile: she
drawing near – heart torn by love-failures – to the source now,
the sustenance. The stranger, waiting; out of exodus and genesis
with demanding words. Between them, issues of time, of history,
the depths of the iced-over, petrified heart. 'I thirst': who, then,
is keeper of the soul in need: he, or she? Between them, between
past and future, the clarity of water in the moment of its
giving, words echoing beyond the sound of words, beyond clanging
of consonant, bird-call of vowel, how the heart, in its taut holding,
wants to yield, to the presence, the immediacy. She, later,
returning home, stumbles, her pitchers full. He
stays, on the ridge of stone, staring down into the deep
till the moon brightens, down there, in the uttermost darkness :

Papyrus

The word, I have discovered, is food for my surviving,
this need to lay down words on strong papyrus, in strait
and patterned lines, hints of love and yearning, and now

this penchant towards sorrowing, for memory is un-
certain, inaccurate, and, like waters, fluid. Words of Yeshua
who sought to slip away, before dawn, to a desert place, to touch
his source and sustenance. For after all, after that mid hour,
my life will not be what it was; what, then, had happened? The word
existence seemed to shift, as boulders shift in a quake, the straight
line of living twisted back upon itself in a kind of anguish,
what we had accomplished suddenly became undone, the
comfortable dark was now backlit by a more aggressive fire –
for he had stood, tears on his cheeks, before the sealed tomb;
he called: and there was a death-silence: I heard a hum

of insects, somewhere the sharp howl of a jackal, an echo
out of Lethe and in the heat of noon my body chilled;
slowly, they unsealed the tomb, stood at its gaping mouth
mute in darkness; the sisters clutched each other, terrified.
He emerged, slow, slow, shrouded in white cotton, like a great
woodcock with folded wings, body camouflaged in snow,
and it was I who called, out of a living hope within me,
fly high! Lazarus, fly! But he stood still: perplexed, perhaps
blinded by the sun, when the sisters moved to him, and the crowd
astounded, cried with a shrill ululation, like flocks of startled
shore-birds until he stood, freed, and moved towards Yeshua
like a lover stepping out in exaltation. I understood there is no such thing
as the ordinary world, that words themselves are not
transparent, and I became, just then, afraid of this man of men :

Mediterranean

Came that day on the beach; Yeshua stood a long while
and spoke, of love, of mercy, of tenderness; and my spirit
sang again. We grew hungry. There he was, frying fish over stones,
with garlic, oil, fresh bread, and I could not figure

from where came all that food. There were sea winds, and each
morsel that we ate spoke benevolence while the ocean, behind us,
murmured its assent. He had his place now in my heart, no, it was
even deeper than the heart. We had come for pleasure, what we took
was the scent of the sea, a sense of comfort mixed with dread,
the sunset pink of flamingos flying over. I remember the new port,
breakwaters, the Roman galleys, new economies; the stranger –
Yeshua – had taken spittle on his fingers and touched the eyes
of a blind man; but Yeshua had mentioned fear and we saw,
beyond the grasses and wild flowers a small group, hostile, gathering :

The Garden

Dusk – the sun going down – threw long shadows across
the ground. He appeared, coming from the valley, and collapsed
on the hard earth; somewhere a bird sang, though the word
'chuckled' came to mind. I remembered Genesis: the Lord God
walking in the garden, time of the evening breezes. An hour
passed; the world darkened further; up in the city
lights flickered. I thought I heard sobbing, even a scarcely
suppressed cry. He rose, and moved, stumblingly, back
towards the wall; I heard voices, protestations. Then he came
to fall again, scrambling on earth as if his bones were fire
and though I sensed rather than saw his body, he was distorted
like limbs of the olive trees. I heard weeping; I heard fingers
scrabbling against ground. Weakness, and failure; embarrassing.
Relief to see the flare of torches coming this way from the city :

The Viewing

When he was harried out to be jeered at, blood-
ugly, rag-scraggly, filthy with sores, I knew
he must be guilty and I was ashamed. He could

scarcely hold himself erect, they jostled him,
there was blood congealing on his face, his
fingers, even on his naked, blistering feet. He had no
hope, he was already stooped amongst the dead.
Like a fool he stayed silent, stubbornly so, though
words could not save him now. This was degradation
before the people, who mocked his agonies, his death,
the ultimate humiliation, for even rats
will creep away to die, in private, in a dark
corner. We knew now that his name would be
forgotten, left with his corpse in merciful oblivion :

Hill of Skulls

(i)

I stood on the slope, at a distance from the other women;
it was done on the Hill of Skulls, dread place, to discourage
thought; high posts planted, waiting for the cross-
branches, the flower, and the fruit, where the dead earth
was rusted over with spilled blood; a little aside –
though within eye-shot – from the city's bustle and indifference.
Miryam, for it must be she, stood propped between strength
and failure, determined mother to the last. I had dreamed
he would put an end to violence. The big iron nails
were not the worst, though the heavy hammer-blows
shuddered the earth and shuddered my heart – it was the body
writhing in agony, chest strained beyond the possible at each
in-breath, out-breath, it was how humankind spits hatred
against its own, the tender-hearted, innocent, the children – but

(ii)

it's how things are, the soldier said, and will always be.
The moments passed, each one dragging as an hour; I tried
prayer, but to whom, or to what? The sky darkening, the groans
lengthening, the screams... He was burning. Near us the cackling
magpies. In the sky, the vultures. The way, he had said,
the truth, the life – is the way then, death? Life, the urgencies
only of the body? And truth, what is truth? His blood
mingling on the earth with blood of the contemned. Love
the final casualty. Clouds blackened; hot winds
blew in across the hill, shadows were dancing wildly
amongst confused noises. He cried out, though rarely. My
tears were silent, copious. I heard a distant, drawn-out
thunder. After such hours he screamed out, died; as if
he had exhaled, with his last breath, all the light and

(iii)

life of the world. Thunderstorms as they took
him down, as I hurried through the streets people
were staggering by, like ghosts. I never felt so
much alone. That was the most muted evening,
night was black and long and I armed myself about
with fires of spitting olive-wood; in the laneways skulked
furtive shapes; I clung, desperately, to the supposed
mercy of time; words had lost essence and would spill
like hot grease. How could the world know he had lived, how
could the word love be redefined? Everything unfinished, all
undone. But I had inks, formed out of soot and oil and tears
and would carve deep in the papyrus. I remember – back then
on the mountainside – he had said: those of singleness of heart
will be blessed, for it is they who will see God :

Sunrise

So clear we had not grasped it: in the giving away of life
you find it. Soon after dawn I was leaning on the stone walls
of the vineyard out beyond the city. There was a well, timbers
covering it; I heard the wood rattling; there was a man
stooping over, reaching for a drink; he saw me, called out
something, waved, and was gone. Tricks of the light, I thought,
the sudden wing-claps of doves distracting. I stayed, fingers
worrying the clay between the stones. I had not even
waved back. Bright this early and I imagined the valley
singing softly. The intimacy of grape-flesh, I thought, the skin
peeled off, the dark wine waiting. The mind can find itself
so foolish, hoping for too much. The quickening of a heart
urgent against grief. Or urgent towards unutterable
joy. And I stood there, stood, baffled again by this one life :

The Turning

After the killing, there was no hope left, nowhere
to turn. We abandoned the city, wondering if we might
get somewhere. Sat, disconsolate, by the river, knowing
how goodness appears and is vanquished before it is
clasped. Wondering if there is a way for mortal beings
to start over. Someone, walking the same path, may offer
wisdom, and insight. Becomes, in the nonce, mediator
between place and non-place, life not-life, death and
not-death. The day advancing, our steps more sprightly,
we would hold to light against the nightfall. That someone…
Logs blown to flames in the hearth; dried fish, olives, figs
and honeyed wine; the ready warmth of love, the torn hands
blessing and breaking bread. What the blood had known
known now in spirit and for truth. And so we turned :

Lydia

I fear onslaughts of foolishness before the end,
the loss of wonder when the mind cools, the wine
ordinary, the bread bread. Do not fear, he said, only
believe. I work to keep the heart open, glory in the once-fire
that will be ash, in reason beyond reason. I work to cherish
the variegated birdsong, the damson flowers blossoming
when they will. That I may ever overflow with Yeshua,
as a jug will overbrim with a wine both sweet and bitter.
I know I will meet him again, the raw wounds of humanity
on his flesh. I remember the sea's edge, when, late evening,
he spoke from the fishing-boat anchored just off-shore: See
and hear as a child, he said, that the deaf hear and the blind
have their eyes opened, the lame walk and the dead rise again
and blessed is the one who does not lose faith in me.

FLY-TYING

I watched him, hooked over the kitchen table,
    the instruments of his heart's desire
ranged before him: tweezers, dubbin, vise;
    materials – feathers, threads, fluffs and beads;

he opened out his folding wallet, his treasury of flies,
    richness beyond delight, all beautiful and murderous.
I, too, inveigled, though on a lesser scale, in my way
    was searching the world's presence for its pulse and throb;

the vegetable garden, after rain, yielded its lush
    pink-red worms I gathered into his old tobacco tin.
Dusk, and he was wading into the lake, he curled
    the fleshly-coloured line onto the water, the chosen flies

vivid as if they lived. I, with stump-rod, twine and worm
    sat by the river pool, watched the cork, dreamed
and – impatient with his patience – slapped at midges.
    Who has long gone into the anima mundi, rest

for the soul, the spirit-wallet filled with all good things,
    peace for the flesh from the flesh's urge, to be and to be
more than it may be here: clay, and thread, bright
    gaud and hook, and consistent disappointment.

FROM THE WINDOW

Almost solstice; on an ice-blue sky the fluffed-wool
dissolving trail of a jet is stitching and unstitching; to-night
there will be stars, sharp as broken ice-glass
and small birds sheltering somewhere, in the earth's care;

here love evolves, through the small events and the remarkable;
you, in the garden, vivid in red windcheater,
your rubber gloves – one yellow, the other blue – as you deal
in clay and mulch, lift the tubers of this late summer's

dramatic dahlias – the bitter-lemon star, the all-hallows-red
Bishop of Llandaff – and lay them out in knotted sausage-shapes
in the tigín to dry; you turn, a moment, towards me, and smile;

the house is quiet, where I sit inside the window, watching,
hearing the vole-like scritch and scratch of my pen, as it turns, turns
to work at the daunting, cosmic whiteness of the page.

THE SPOILING FRUIT

They dumped the black Ford Prefect
in the drain, down by the hawthorn hedge. In spring
the first white blossoms flourished round it; then
the spread of dogwoods, the bramble push-and-reach

played over it and under, and in a very few years
the old Ford Prefect became root and swell and yield.
Now under the apple trees the reddest apples, wasps
gorging on the spoiling fruit, and sunlight

battening on the whitewashed wall; there gleams
a difficult beauty, the harshest sweetness, and grey
vulgar abundance in the neglected yard; at night
dimly visible clouds play games with the blossoming

stars; vixen feasts beside her cubs, invisible visitors
at the compost heap. At dawn, at noon, at night
we celebrate what the world has gifted us, the sorrows
of imperfection, the joys of tenderness; our prayers

to the Lord Creator: he is our peace, we are his poem.

BY-THE-WIND SAILOR

Send forth your spirit and they shall be created,
and you will renew the face of the earth.

In the beginning, breath agitated like the breeze,
the stitched sheet rippled like a foal, and the home-built

'Unsafe' safe, craft for the now, shivered beyond the stones;
wind slight, the bog-lake standing at ease. We are children,

always, attentive to the breath. Braced
for the extraordinary.

*

In the enclosed garden there is the high proud mastery
of hollyhock and delphinium, of soft-pink rose and lupin

where bumble-bee and variegated Eden-coloured butterflies
speak peace and silence and the passion of earthen things.

Outside the walls there is the wilful human violence, darkness
of the common soul, of the quick and the departed.

Belief, with its creel of ritual and mystery, becomes
difficult. The walls are coloured with the figures of dread:

dragons and demons, the cockerel betrayal of the Christ,
barbarian terror abroad. Our breath is prayer, lifting our spirits

to the breeze. We sing our hymns to the candle-flame
and sink, all of us, refugees, into moth-silent night.

*

The mind, mornings, waits scraggy as the heron's nest
high in the ruffled treetops;

the boy in me wants to be an old-timer
riding a palomino across high sierras, inhaling orange dust

with vultures circling on the wheels of air above,
wants to be the suave and grease-haired

still-young and disillusioned toreador sipping chilled
Marqués de Cáceres rosé wine on a Toledo terrace.

*

You I think of as a bird, of a white so pure you skim
to invisibility; you are the high-pitched buzz

of the hover-fly, bog cotton in sunlight and a gusting wind,
a wavering of white butterflies struggling towards flight;

you are the Portuguese man o' war, the sea raft
wafting on the surface of the ocean, you are primordial

waters, as if the words might come *ex nihilo*, a wind
blowing across the deep, making a covenant with being.

*

Something of Yeshua/Jesus has left its caul
in my flesh, my skull is riven with a blood-feud darkness

like the painfilled leftover reek in an abandoned beehive cell.
Child years were a haze of fragrances: frankincense, myrrh,

the perfumes of papa God's bazaars;
the thurible, with its chains, its censer, its incense boat

was a charmed Aladdin's lamp. I must be contented now
with homeliness from those deckled years – with peace

before high windows, wet sunlight coming through in shards
like hollyhock and soft-pink rose, Chagall-blue lupin;

I find acceptance now amongst benevolent spectres
present beside me; and am contented with the beloved

lately dead who drift away from my mourning into the bright,
woodbine-scented morning of their all-knowing.

*

Sometimes the words caught steady brightness
though more often they languished in an under-the-stairs

dust-dark. Braced for the extraordinary I held belief
in sunlight and sacrament, in white sheets strung

along blue skipping-rope, hoisted high in sea-shore winds;
I prayed for an outpouring, *coram Deo*, the keen presence

of the breath of life, the way the Spirit came whispering fire
to the churches, that Spirit, more gannet perhaps than dove,

that white-flash down-dive welcome and daunting. Years
I have been cassocked in darkness, surpliced in light –

held safe in spite of repeated under-the-skin infidelities –
my world like the glass snow-globe that – when you turned it

upside-down – sent a tiny full-rigged ship in gentle motion
across a wavering sea. I think, now, of that innocence, moments

like a small child's flowered wellingtons splashing
on the sky that mirrors itself in a snow-melt pool.

*

I walked, one clarifying day, the pebbled and billion-shelled
shore of the lake where you knelt, Yeshua, at dawn, preparing fish,

rewriting the landscape, redressing our suppositions
and all our certainties. You, fox on the margins, Jesus, alert

and espied. I inhaled the moon over Hermon that was duck-down white
and I drank cold beer on the shore of Kinnaret

while Israeli jets jarred the sky in their war-games,
above you – gentle and all-suffering – still – the Christ.

*

In the plum-blue out-there darkness
and high above the intently-watching towers –

in slow ballet: the galaxies, driven and intent like those
myriads of by-the-wind-sailors on the seas and can you sense

the fissures and glaciations down the faces of the planets
that are, up there, in the dance, serene. I am at home

with heather-tuft and turf-bank, with curlew-call
and the constant love-nothings murmured to the coast

by soft-capped waves. There is an old fragility
in the lace-like edges of all things, how the solitary haw

(with its invisible, roseate angels, its prickly littlepeople)
is shot through with ivy. Tonight the constellations

will appear in another quarter of the sky, my bones
will singe with sentience of seasoning, of now, of geologic time.

I would share, down here, in the gentle communion of saints,
as the quizzical light the moon has focused on the park

will be gone by morning, the trail the vixen left through the grasses
will vanish soon, earth shriven again by her golden ochre light.

*

I watch out now over Lake Michigan; in me there is
a willingness to let go, a readiness to open to the pulse

that will touch on silence beyond silence, where word
has taken root, to reach a faith beyond faith where Word –

unheard – responds. There was a day above Keem Bay –
can you paint a beach in cobalt blue? – for there they were,

innumerable, by-the-wind-sailors, flung ashore by the high tide;
it was an image of sky, cerulean blue and shivering, a whole

testament of ages, of life and blessed passivity, words
of the world's dramas, its epics and illustrated books

where we, at our very best, discover ourselves, too,
mendicants, loving the absence that will come to save us.

*

On the hundred and somethingth floor of the Willis Tower
it is hard to breathe; you may step out here onto the skydeck,

you are straw-in-the-wind a while, open to it, and scared;
you are beyond your capacity to be and only Spirit

keeps you exposed, open to the demands of word and Word
till your being brims and overflows. You are urged back

to earth, at the sea's edge, and the spirit sighs within you;
here the black rocks are charred with weed, sheen with sea-water –

a seal, lifting its great attentive eyes, comes curious towards you,
its sleek eel-sinewy body graced under the surface, then

turns and dives back into its element, leaving you solitary again.
You have learned it, this-world wonder and danger, reach, withdrawal;

you are by-the-wind Sailor: deep blue, amethyst and cobalt,
small spirit-sail that lifts and carries you and you do not know

from where it comes nor in what station it will abandon you;
there will be disturbance at sea, touching on islands,

and millions of them – *vellela vellela* – moved by the breath,
open to it, will stir with a shiver of anticipation, breeze

soundfull, and in unison, like words that are gathering
in a chant of praise, or in a psalm, an *Eloi Eloi…* and you

are driven by gusts, gasped or long-haul, towards shore
till at last, shockingly, the whole beach is written over blue.

OLD BONES

I, John, I was on the island called Inishmurray...

There was a sense of Genesis to it, Alpha moment,
morning sun over the waters off Mullaghmore, boat-engine idling
while we sat on fishing-boxes
and relished the yapping of waves against the hull.

Benbulben in the distance, slopes of sun and shadow,
sheltering Ireland's poet under her wings.
The castle, Classiebawn, loomed
as a dark landmark above the cliff, and we knew

these waters brimmed, not long ago, with broken thwarts
and exploded faith. For this is Ireland, holding her wars,
her poets, her ruins and her rains, and the holy islands
where we, the curious, come to pray.

*

Outside the harbour wall we pitched in unexpected swell,
Atlantic Ocean spray
blessing us with salt. Our touching on the island was
uneasy, without dock or quay, only the black rocks

slippery with weed and sea-wet. Herring-gulls barked
like guard-dogs and a kestrel,
fast as a prayer, flew by. I scaled a rock-trail through thistles
where the testy ghosts

wished to be left in peace. To this abandonment, friars came
centuries after the Christ, to forge
salvation, built rock altars, beehive cells, stone churches,
piled up their cursing-stones to keep

*

women and fiends at bay…
What is it, then, of sea and sky and island,
of isolation and self-denial, that has left its caul
in my flesh and soul that I come

to scavenge here for understanding?
The black-backs watch, sharp-eyed and silent, shuffling
on the dry-stone walls, like monks restless in choir.
Within the ramparts of the enclosure

I sit, lost and at home. Out on the headland an old man plays,
off-tune, a slow lament:
'*an raibh tú ag an gcarraig*' and the sea responds:
a sigh and a withdrawal.

A SINGULAR VOICE

The old font still stands: back of the church, in a dry
stillness. I have grown old, imperceptibly, a little

cranky, but remembering how once, here, unmeasured
gifts and demands were offered me. Safe passage.

I have since learned I was not born with darkness
shadowing my soul, nor was there shame laid on me

from millennia before my birth. I am Yeshua, / Jesus,
being held, then, and now, naked, in the river, angels

hovering about me: (Ted and Nanna, Jo and Don, Patricia,
big brother Declan) until the water-god released me

into order, giving me a name. Islandman, creature
of the seemly earth, here at the boundary shore of being.

They dried me off, called me Christian, wrapped me
in the whitest shawl, brought me out where thorn bushes

stood up bare in winter frost, to the potency of love
and a blessed creation. I sense they may be gathering again,

near the fount; I offer small lights and pray I may be granted *safe*
passage one more time. Outside I heard the lingering

whistle-cry of the whimbrel, a singular voice from that old
migratory bird, calling from the marshes down along the shore.

THE HUMMING TOP

Mother knelt by my crib and prayed, and I
was forgiven the sins of the day;
she blew out the flame, left me
and I was not scared of demon-dreams or the dark;

crossing my arms over my breast, I remembered
the spinning-top left downstairs, how its pictures
of horses and parrots and caravans
blurred into yellows and reds; I slept, the spinning

globe in my mind, and all of the creatures.
Though I knew how beautiful the world is,
was aware that both child and adult weep
sometimes, and though I saw how the white-fronted geese

labour through the ice-green twilight,
and watched how the robin comes brazen
to the garden seat, no one had given me
the words. And because I sensed that the dream was me

and not me, I cried too, I laughed
and made signs, knowing already
how the great world turns, and spins,
the colours fuse, and the humming goes on and on.

THE FLOWERING

In the convent halls, religious order;
in the nuns' garden, a riotous abundance;

in the parlour she is offering a tray, with coffee, tea,
biscuits plain and chocolate-chip;

at the garden's edge, the boiler room – boots
with soft clay drying to a grey daub – and the instruments:

trowel and secateurs, gardening gloves and kneelers. Then
she is out – forget-me-not-blue apron over navy habit –

and she moves, like a ward sister, working to tend,
to prune, to coax; kneels, as if in prayer, 'concerning

the times and seasons', evening primrose, flowering
sage, Siberian wall-flowers. The high iris stands,

an extravagantly coiffed princess, by the sapphire-coloured rose;
nearby, flowers she cares for, with names like those of exotic

foreign traders: alium, astrantia, delphinium; they lift
in homage to kindly, ministering hands, hands that fold, often,

in pleading. To-night she will sit a while, after Vespers, alone
on the wrought-iron garden seat, and will be glad –

thinking of bridal bouquet, corsage, ring –
that soon she will stumble away into that old, singular garden

to meet, at last, the Bridegroom, to yield
to the drag of origins within, to her own, certain, flowering.

LINDISFARNE

To-night the sea, out in the obdurate dark, shifts
in obedience, the seals hauling themselves out
onto the long shelf of sand, in their own slick nudity,

shifting, too, in a restlessness of seals, their plangent
hymns to one another carrying into the weave of human
dreams and half-sleep, into the flesh of the long dead

floating in dust of the universe in soul-nakedness.
We are young a while, and seek sanctuary, Lindisfarne,
where saintly ghosts glide by, their voices distant

as the loon's song out over the ocean, and close
as the curlew's call purling from the fens.
The North Sea's force spends itself in spume

and the herring-boats lie safe above the tide-line.
I seek a haven that is not loneliness but a table
set with a white linen nappe and laid for four.

We will be old a time, allowed some scope, hold
that the poems shaping themselves in the soul's sanctum
may stay the waves a while as they call out to our God.

I AM

I left the pew, slowly, following
men and women old as I, and older;
we are cautious now, we – communion

of the living – holding on. I took
in my palm the white, the cosmic bread
and placed it on my tongue, took a sip

of the earth-sweet and bitter wine;
amen, I said, amen. So am I guest
at the crude table of the Upper Room,

am Jewish-Christian, Hellenist, I am
Greco-Roman, Byzantine, bear on my tongue
full two millennia of a difficult history,

the proving – down a long bleak tunnel
scarce candle-lit – of the original mandate
of the Alpha, the Omega Christ.

CUTHBERT: A LIFE

Through chill and warmth in the low hills
he learned the music timid sheep respond to:
that soft and ululating boy-song

of artlessness and sweet grass, a high-pitched
guardian air that drove the falcons
far from the brimming harmlessness of lamb.

He was taken from innocence too young.
At twelve, apprenticed to a saint. Life
over. Harshness was a creed and habitude.

He walked the earth on muddy, rutted trails,
tramping hillock, hollow and lane, handling
immensities. By offal pits and slurries

he confessed our immortality. Shepherding.
Solicitous, not for this life, but for treasure
in heaven. What then, Cuthbert,

of the poor and ignorant,
intimates of this world of grace and ugliness,
what of the body, dear and beautiful,

what of the Christ of banquets, what can you say
of God's most good creation? And what
of eros, and the waiting arms of the love-lorn Christ?

THE RATTLE OF OLD BONES: INISHBOFIN

The men were standing outside the church, hearing
Mass; dark Sunday suits, flat caps and cautionary pipes;

serious men, one eye on weathers, one on neighbours,
easing this hour between worlds, jocular, strong-jawed

and firm-standing, like erratics. In St Colmán's
ruined monastery, sheep safely graze; in waves off-shore

the fishing-boats chant, in old Gaelic, timeworn psalms
of the wild-weltering sea. In deepest hour of night, the bones

of monks, slaughtered in the malevolent invasions
of the Vikings, set themselves to their eight-hand reels,

there is joy through communion of saints, out under the light
of the moon – spine-slides, skeletal slip-jigs, the hysterical

laughter of skulls. 'Woe is me,' saith the book, 'for my soul
hath fainted, because of the saints that are slain.'

BILBERRY BELLS AND ASPHODEL

This is the yellow house where the dead
return, rehearsing their old delights, bemoaning the loss
of rough-red Lifebuoy soap against the skin,

or the heat against her knuckles as Grandmother Nora toasts
bread on the long fork held to the fire; Grandfather Ted
misses the drool of melting butter along the hot

potato boxty cake, and oh! how Father
longs for the slow-walk down to the well to dip the jug
with its blue-rose pattern, and hear the first

flush-slap of water into the dinted, off-white pail.
You too, brother, do you sense it, sunlight
flickering on fern, on bilberry bells and asphodel,

those wander-lust mornings we heard the hum of insects
and the fuzzy sounds of bees busy inside the blossoms?
And do you remember – now that you too

have gone into the world of light – how we sat on our hard
three-legged stools and sang, there in the corner
by the high fuchsia and the rhododendron, *All things bright*

and beautiful? Will you come back, now, to pick up once more
words of the yellowhammer's song, that smell from pages
of the new reader with the odour of apples baking in the kitchen,

while Mother's welcoming arms waited for an embrace?
How fine then the weight of knowledge, like featherfall,
and we, content in our unknowing, in our young otherselves!

ACCOMPANIED

The ascent is easiest at the beginning;
six men, strong labourers,
right-shoulder left-shoulder,
take the weight; bog-path, ground rising already,

passing by the *cillín* of the lost children,
big waves bullying in
against the low-cliff home-ground
this side the mountain,

home ground too – rest eternal – the other side.
This human stream, dark-frothed,
rises slowly, against nature;
soft, almost-animal, coughs and cries

and women, shawled, huddling.
Pause;
lower the coffin carefully,
to shift the ache in the bearers' flesh;

build a small cairn of stones where the coffin touched,
a station; six fresh bearers.
On, over heath-hummock, steep bank and treacherous earth;
only the dead man peaceful and unwary.

There will be, at the top, a longer pause,
a larger cairn, a lingering look back
over the long curve of the bay, the sea breaking
audibly still, the deep past incalculable.

Beads are told, a mind-numbing, repetitious drone.
Station; six more labouring men,
left-shoulder right-shoulder,
for the more difficult descent. There are men below,

at rest on pick and shovel,
watching up at the dismal sacrament that moves
like a bleak and bog-black
sluggish watercourse, inaudible from below;

there are gulls' cries, a distant
curlew calling, the monkish
hooded crows kraaking,
and sleek black slugs mating under the rain.

ON KEEL BEACH

I bring my demons down to the sea-shore
and loose them amongst unsettling sea-rolled stones;

here I stand firm against the storm-winds, cherishing
the buffeting and the surging power of the waves, the delicate

seam-stitching needlework of receding water. Wrapped tight
in my great-coat, hands in pockets, I release the memories

and the winds will carry them away: *what
are the wild waves saying?* I sing, in the mind's recess,

sing with my brother, appeasing parents in the old sitting-room,
world gracious and at ease, turf-fire vibrant in the grate, slow,

sentimental duet – *that ever amidst our playing
I hear but its low, lone song.* Tattered along the tide-line,

refuse of the ocean: bladderwrack and wing-kelp, toxins
of our human desecration, and there – amongst the cans

and plastics – the rotting carcass, the sodden feathers
of a gannet. Out across the sea, beyond my ken

but within my prayers, sorrows and slaughters of this
still-young century; Tikrit, Mosul; the heart is wrenched

by the barbarities; Babylon and the rivers,
Tigris, sluggish now with military waste,

and the Euphrates, blue river, its waters
drying up, trickling towards a desolate sea. And I remember

father, mother, in their easy-chairs by the fire,
Granny by the window, humming, her knitting-needles

clacking their steady rhythms: *Brother, I hear no singing,*
'tis but the rolling wave. Away to my left the great, dark cliffs,

cathedral-proud, the fulmar soaring; where father fished,
spinning from the rocks for mackerel, his taut and urgent

longing, evident. And I see them, too, the children,
wretchedly clothed, in the wind-blown tents for refugees, filled

landscapes of them, snow falling, severe frost holding;
their eyes are dulled and unblinking, watching. My brother

is at peace now in the Queen of Heaven cemetery, the small
many-coloured whirling windmills humming loss. I turn

for home, old man cold and dry-eyed, remembering.
Yes! the song concluded, *but there's something greater*

that speaks to the heart alone. The voice of the great Creator
dwells in that mighty tone. And the wind turns, and the tide.

THEN AND NOW

He – abandoning the inland sureties of the Christian Brothers –
    came, for the first time, to island; took up fishing from the high

rocks beyond Purteen, stirred by the wonder of the Atlantic; I,
    then unthought of, am there, too, on the cliff-edge near him, waiting.

She – native to island – was picnicking, with Patricia, on the strand,
    a basket with sandwiches, a rose-red wine and Waterford

cut-glass tumblers; they have been laughing, youth and promise
    copious as the blue sky. I, then unthought of, am there, too,

watching from the breaking waves, waiting. Now I stand, sea's edge,
    stunned at the knowledge of my ageing, he, and she, and Patricia,

decades gone into the ocean of all unknowing. And since
    time itself is imagination, and then is now, now then – I call to them

from where I sit, pensive and waiting, January rain slanting down
    and vanishing into the heaving sea, melding with its waves, its breakers.

Or I could, perhaps, spend all there is of after-life
walking the road between Dooagh village
and the beach at Keem, flexing the spirit-muscles,
strengthening the spirit-bones. Sometimes a telephone pole,
blown over in a Force 10, will lie down across the path,
communication wires from the island to the raucous world

tangled like fishing-gut. Here I have most nearly found
the source of the being of Ireland, my soil, my sky,
my sea, my here-ness. I will have learned the thousand words
that said amen to the thousand weathers I had grown
familiar with, learned to hold my breath when witnessing
the rare serene light shining over the bay, the sea

a delicate shamrock green, translucent, and the waves
fingering the slow notes of a Schubert lullaby on Keel strand.

ICARUS

Young man of the Cretan uplands, downlands,
of the labyrinthine rutways of mountain villages,
olive-groves, goats, of the gaunt, bell-ringing sheep –

he would fly, as I would, in the relish of bounteous grace.
Whipped by the wind at first, as fear will fling you,
then mastering it, the shoulder-muscles jousting;

then it was the light, blinding him as he topped
Mount Ida and the White Mountains, the island below
like rags and patches clawed and torn, strewn about.

When the blindness eased he saw Daedalus, maker-Father,
cautious on the up-draughts beneath, but by now the son
was master, beyond fear, beyond vision, climbing

on the upbeam of the sky, feathered arms spread
cruciform and soaring; so high he saw the earth revolving
and time itself like a vineyard fruiting and dying back.

So high, at last, so cold, pain suffusing, he was suffering,
punished for robbing the world of gravity, till what was glory
froze in him, bones, sinews, becoming iron, and he plummeted,

bloodless, over the utmost horizons of our history.

TRIPLE H

Sometimes I think of them, the saints:
their sutured habits and ghost-white cinctures,

eyes wide-open upwards in a static rapture, their floating
inches above the flagged floor in cantilevered ecstasy,

and the words we use: inimitable, righteous, the
un-mortals: Hippolytus, Helena, Hyacinth...

Often I think of them, the saints:
writing outside themselves of themselves inside –

Hopkins in his long, unglamorous suffering,
small snappy man in a misery of muscled language;

Herbert, his consciousness of dustworth,
his tentative but eager treaty of love;

and Heaney, witness to the gracefulness of the frames
of dailiness, enamoured of the possible, the worth

of next-door otherness and the allsorts savouring of words:
these, O God, your dead, your un-mortals.

THE MEDITERRANEAN

Here, in the fields of mercy, the spirits of those
hundreds, thousands
of children, women, men, come brushing by me,
fleeing the human hornets

of fanaticism and greed, though too many have found
quiet in the bitter depths
of the Mediterranean Sea – who will, one day, rise again
to the surface, children, women, men

with psalms accusatory on their lips. Now I stand
on the sheltered island coast, the sea
brushing the shore softly; I am awed by the yellow-linen
stillness of evening primrose, and by butterflies

storming the buddleia, while the star-shaped
golden-white geranium is wilting
in its pot. Ageing body, dull brain perplexed,
I am startled by the scream of a black-back

carrion gull and can image the over-crowded tubs
and rusting wrecks out
on perilous seas; I know that I – faced
with such human turbulence – am runt and reckling,

am no commander nor able-bodied seaman to steer
the desperate into harbour. Knowing,
as I do, the lyric impulse touches on strange borders
and is entranced by mystery, affecting little.

REFUGEE

This, then, is the Christ.
They named him Alan, Alan Kurdi.
He is three years old.

Red T-shirt, short-sleeved;
navy-blue shorts, shoes navy-blue.
He has been washed ashore.

He lies, face down, on the wet shingles.
He is helpless; he has been helpless
all his life. He was obedient

in everything.
He was lifted aboard a crowded dinghy.
He had few words.

He is the word.
In him all things were created. And in him
all things hold together.

I would send word, before I go into that
blank otherness, its silence and obscurity,
that I might hear King's College Choir sing to me

Allegri's *Miserere*; then, to cheer me, Barbara Hendricks
with Mozart's bright and vesper-sweet *Laudate Dominum*;
followed, because I have learned that it is so, by Vivaldi's

Nulla in mundo pax sincera. Finally, as they lay me down,
the Soggy Bottom Boys might choir: *I'm in the Jailhouse Now.*
When I have caught my breath in the New Land

I'll ask my Christ if I might spread my condor wings
and soar, soundlessly, through space and time to find –
April 13, seventeen forty-two, Dublin, Fishamble Street,

where I, amongst the gentry and the commoners, may fold
my wings and hear, its first time sung, *I know that my
Redeemer liveth...* and sense at last all yearning's done.

NAMING OF THE BONES
London, June 2017

I looked up and saw you, your distorted body
writhing again in agony. There is a season, the Big Book says,

a time to die, a time to weep, and a time for peace;
no one, it says, can understand what is happening under the sun.

I saw the bare breast heaving, that once beautiful breast;
I hurt for you, for your beloved once beautiful, body, each twist or twitch,

each reach and wrench adds to the fire in your flesh
and bones. I plead to creator lover God for you, to ease your pain,

to mother you. I wince once more at the bitter-spittle angers
of humankind: the blunted iron nails driven through your caring hands,

your tender feet; so that impossible you hang from them,
and stand on them; the muscles cramp and spasm, and your face,

so beautiful once, is contorted with spit and ugliness, with
blood and sweat and tears. Today, my Christ, June 14, twenty-seventeen,

Grenfell Tower in London was engulfed in flames; inestimable
furnace, suffering unbearable. A child appears for a moment, at a window

of the sixteenth floor, a moment only, frantic, waving:
to a not-there-saviour; you? We hurt, my Christ, we hurt. Why is our spittle

hot with bitterness? Words, the Big Book says, can be
wearisome, a chasing after wind. And yet... the world breaks. The world

re-forms. But the beautiful body breaks, and yields.
Yearning and grief trouble us. At the heart of it. You. Hurting.

LIKE THE DEWFALL

[Note: 'Like The Dewfall' – The French composer Olivier Messiaen (1908–1992) wrote a suite of seven pieces for two pianos, composed and performed in 1943 during the Nazi Occupation of Paris. He called the suite 'Visions de l'Amen', 'Visions of the Amen'; Messiaen describes the music as seven visions reflecting the lives of those who say 'Amen', accepting the details of their existence with gratitude. I owe a debt of gratitude to the book *Visions of Amen*, by Stephen Schloesser, Professor of history at Loyola University, Chicago. The book is published by Wm. B. Eedermans Publishing Co., Michigan, 2014]

A BOY-CHILD

Amen of Creation

There is a boy, urging a child-sized US army jeep
around a dew-damp Achill Island yard,
pedalling and steering, and the small stones bump
the khaki-green, star-marked plaything;

a cockerel scolds loudly as he cock-steps along the wall,
battle and stand-off
between cockerel and boy being everyday events
of moment. Distant, familiar and unfamiliar, that child,

there where the pine-tree grove was bounded
by flowering escallonia bushes, where robin,
thrush and blackbird sang, where the Angelus bell
told over the Incarnation. Noon, he is in the parlour,

at the piano, much against his will: battling the scales,
the fingering, the sharps, the flats...
Tempo! time! time! the music-mother calls;
on the lacquered lid the tick-tock-tick of the metronome,

while the world turns outside and the fuchsia is in bloom.
Adagio, cantabile, softly, softly;
from this time out it will all be *crescendo, allegretto* – and yet!
amen to the music, and amen to the universe,

– from cockerel to hump-back whale, from quark to galaxy –
amen to the Christ-child, chortling in the crib, new-earthed
heart of creation, who is, who was, who is coming-to-be;
to sustained harmony of the spheres: amen! *Pianissimo.* Begin.

*

They said that the stork had flown, late,
    through the night sky, in over Bunnacurry; but he

was approaching the age of reason and knew it had to be
    Big Seán heron, scrawny-bodied and heavy-winged,

creaking his wagon-self back to the bog-pools and
    water-lily ponds of the lower mountain. In school,

the Brothers harped always on the fall, loading on fresh minds
    the burdens of original sin and guilt, as if they –

young-lads in short trousers and fraying ganzies –
    had been mitching in the garden when the ancestors

bit into fruit that left chalk-dust forever in the mouth.
    They fought, as boys will fight – bloody noses, purpled eyes –

and they raided the smaller orchards of the island, though
    sensing there were deeper purposes, and they'd learn them.

*

Bog-boy, they called him, for his dreaming
among the cuttings; he was at home

up on the turf-bank, down in the cutaway,
moorland breathing in its variegated and sepia

ease. He loved the world-berating
sweet-bird wheatear, the sudden snipe,

soprano trilling of the skylark; loved
the dragonflies, their wings, those forms

of a polychrome antiquity. He tip-toed over
the daffodil innocence of bog-asphodel, fingered

the white-fluff stuff of bog-cotton tufts, embraced
the lean-to wigwam footings, the turf-sods

wet with the life-sap of earth, and rain, and timelessness.
His delight, to be barefoot for a while,

squishing the ooze of mud between his toes, hearing
the distant haling sounds of the ocean. Knowing himself

in sunshine, to be one with the life of the peat-bog,
had come upon him insidiously as the dewfall,

and in dusk-light, under a peach-soft moon
with stars bright against bright on the blue-grey

mantle of the sky, he sensed himself to be
cell of the cosmos, fleck on the foam of the flux.

*

To each beginning its new ignorance, a world
to know, a shore to step out from. Discovering
once more, before night turns full dark, how light
has shifted from clouded blue and how the heart

is worrying again at the impossible mystery, each of us
being a mere creature, of history, of the variable, on-going
flow. The road out of Bunnacurry back towards Keel
holds its own importance; critical, too, are the steps

down from the pier to the mud-flats when the tide is out;
like ribs of the unearthed dinosaur, the black
timbers and spars of the trawler that has been sinking

year by year into the digesting belly of estuary while clear
water from the mountain spring darkens under turf-banks
and meets and merges with the salt arteries of ocean.

*

He was drawn by the sounds of small streams in flood after rain;

eels, over the stones, eased past; honey-coloured trout, little-bodied,
        beautiful and supple, fair-flecked, held themselves, mouths
        gulping, steady against the downflow;

the joy of shaping a flesh-saucer with two hands to drink, supping
        like a stag or mistle-thrush;

fishing in the deeper pools, watching a cork jig-jogging, catching
      mostly nothing (and pleased at that), but holding the delight
      forever;

the moment, kneeling, gazing down into the purest water, hearing
      the Angelus bell ring its insistent message from the monastery,
      turning to look up and querying – *angelus?* thinking what
      an angel might be,

till the wet and cold against his knees told him again of flesh.
      Knowing later, when smitten at last with the Christ, he had been
        always
      turning, unconsciously, to face him, flinching already
      from the embrace.

   *

It begins, too, with a slight
fingernail-pittering against the panes,
that spittle-spatter knocking
of the smallest hailstones
out of the largest sky;

he will press his face to the window,
in delight; the world, skirt-gathering
against all things standing,
will relish its dance of grey-dark
light across the fields.

Ebullience, creation says,
is of the essence, fecundity
from vacuity towards wholeness.
The greenfinch comes, little quantum
of luminous greens, beak feverish

at the feeder; cosmogenesis is the word
– a few seeds scattered by its hunger
onto snow-softened ground. The sun,
emerging, will cast a wet
shivering along the verges

and a truck, passing, will make
a loving, hissing sound. Knowing
the beating of the heart of matter,
resplendence out of centre into centre,
he will be vigilant, and fused.

*

Come stand awhile, here, at the outermost edge
of the world, the end and the beginning;

Ireland, Atlantic weathers, the cliff face sheened
with rain; sunlight glints off the schist diamonds,

a dusty dribble of stones splitters down into the sea.
Here the child knelt, on the window-seat, gazing out

at hard, inhibiting elements; on the upstairs landing,
in a cut-glass vase, Delft-blue and linen-white hydrangeas

stood in autumnal light; he could hear grandmother,
who dressed in black, sobbing behind her bedroom door.

The child was learning that there are stations of sadness
on the long journey, from *introibo* towards *amen*, because,

she told him, years of dreams appeared to her, this late,
to roost like bats from branches of diseased elms. Stand,

this precious moment, on the bridge at Achill Sound; watch
all the oceans of the world come teeming out of Blacksod Bay

to roar and crush through the gullet of the Sound;
at high tide there will come quiet, a still point, before the turn,

when all the oceans of the world come thrashing back
as if all cosmic being must depend upon it. His, then,

is the music of island. But sometimes there is another music,
in the great hall, that moves him; two dressed in black are seated,

edged, on black piano stools; there is a background
of indeterminate cloth, grey-black; the auditorium stilled,

a few small lights mark exit; two grand pianos are standing
poised, great wings spread. This will be Messiaen, *Visions*

of Amen, each piano challenging the other, each holding
to cliff and crossing, the beginning, and the end. Taut

understanding for the child, like walking barefoot over
bulwark stones, winds crying, while out at sea the whitest

gannets dive; on the strand, he can hear the calls
of oystercatchers, their black and white, their blood-red dagger-bills.

*

Times he played, at a neighbour's sorrow-house,
out in the backyard where hens –
Rhode Island Red and Leghorns – stepped
in slow and skirty busyness

across the hen-shit-spattered ground,
close to the black lake of the sweet-singing birds. No
loveliness to the place, merely
stories of a father who left for easier fallows and did not

return. The sons
fought with stony fists to dim the shame in their own eyes,
the daughter sat in listlessness,
watching the dog – dirt clotted through his hairs –

scratch at himself with fury. Always
the fox, and the dawnlight scattering of feathers,
while the mongrel stretched in the ashes, and a light
shone beneath the picture of a fading Sacred Heart.

Noon and the boys' frayed shirts
were hand-scrubbed and hung over a thorn bush
to dry. Hen-woman made small money
selling eggs and tending graves,

watched the bus each evening and kept the table set:
plate and cup and saucer sporting
a painted house and the word *home* inscribed in blue,
with egg-cup and tarnished pewter apostle spoon.

THE MONASTERY

Amen of the Stars and Planets

The road across the island has been widened;
late in the year the holiday caravans, the campers,

will have drifted home. If you pass this way, pause
at the turn by the new school; find a mild mid-morning

offering merely mistings of rain. Draw your car in
where the gateway pillars have long been overgrown

with trailing shrubbery; you will find a new,
though rickety gate opening on a laneway. Bring

quiet in your heart. Close the gate carefully against the world
and walk. Perhaps you, too, are searching for fount

and fostering, have learned that they drift away
like the many-rainbowed bubbles of your childhood days.

*

You stand now
on an island upon an island where you may find again
you are not an integer, unit among units, here you may
lose yourself in richer being,

new-world-old,
rediscover wholeness and a purpose to your days. Start
down the sandy, stony lane, watching for mud and puddles.
The rhododendron bushes

form wild patternless curtains
on either hand; a breeze brushes the leaves that glisten still
with this morning's dewfall. Come to the smaller gate,
halfway along,

where the boy
entered the two-room school that was and is not.
Where he suffered the boyish challenges at real or wished-for
injuries, wet finger touched to the cheek,

like a glove flung down
at the feet of nobility; wars have always been part of it,
the bully ignorant but counting on his fists. Always,
the extravagance

of the rhododendron blooms,
the dark and sprawling branches and the earth
littered with petals, stirred something in him, a sense
of remotest loss, an emptiness

compounded
with a joyfilled wonder. He, young anchorite, musing
in the dim light that fell through leaf and branch, was
for long, delicious moments,

at peace
with the instances of body. Creation was part of it
and it, all of it, was part of him; being, and being there,
sufficient, it was fullness, it was world.

*

The sun shines on playing fields where seagulls
bicker over crumbs; the window is a little dusty
and tantalising in its height; the walls are rich

with charts of a pastel simplicity, and one big-faced
clock, portentous, swings its pendulum, slowly, too
slowly. Boys tough and fragile, practising swagger,

hold faith with complex workings of the adult
catechisms and stored economies. He learned
that words could grow, long-stemmed and flourishing,

from the ends of his fingers and form patterns
on a white field. Today it is ruin, roofless,
gable-ends crumbling, stone gnawed and blackening,

briars burgeoning where a door should be, and only
the persecuting winds come crowding through
the tumbled walls and rubble. Barbed wire will hold you

back from the mess of muck and sploshes, the starved
grass, thistles, the rushes. He will be standing there
for ever, at that margin, watching out, staring in.

*

He was sent to the monastery, late in the day, for milk;
a half-mile of open road, between deep ditches;

it was, in the late seasons, miserere time, a nervous rush
down the dark lane to the lit side-window where

Brother Cassius filled up the can. Fear of the Lord,
they said, is the beginning of wisdom, that Lord

who numbered all the stars and had assigned them names.
Fear now was darkness, terror and dismay, the world

black, like the raven and her young, cackling. His mind
crackled with images, the *danse sauvage* of Mars and Mercury

and Pluto over the blacked-out ballroom floor of space:
madmen, werewolves, devils and Cloven-Hoof himself

reaching for him… and he prayed to the God who holds
the oceans within bounds, who feeds the young of ravens

when they cry out in their nests… He ran, marking
tempo, élan and repos, rise and fall, air and road,

a drum-beat heart-beat between the intervals of silence.

*

Once, in the guest parlour of the monastery, two
grand pianos, winged and elegant, like seraphim;
on the pastel-coloured walls, stylized pictures:
Francis of Assisi and Anthony of Padua, lives
dedicated to their this-world other-world Christ.
Under shaky spotlights, the pianists; in the shadows
the guests, bemused, in feast day best, and smitten.
Mild applause. The pianists bow and settle. Two
fussed page-turners, the music of Messiaen furious
as thunder-burst, the harmony and counter-harmony
of creation, comet-falls of chords, chromatics, scales,
fingers and wrists of the priest-like bodies of the pianists
pre-occupied by sacrament. The guests all sitting, strained,
half-stifled coughs, a little self-conscious shuffling,
while above it all, in the night air, the monastery bell
waits silent, poised and ponderous in its louvered tower.

*

You must move on, there are further gates to open.
At lane's end you will find relicts of greater trees,
elms, oaks… ragged as scarecrows. To your right,

arthritic remains of an orchard, straggle apple-trees
with bunched fists of fruit, yellowing and bitter,
weeds rampant and cluttering around the roots.

Among fallen stones, seek out echoes of the soul-full
prayers; sparrow and robin watch you, singing hymns
that have not wavered. Pass on, by the hollowed-out

windowless dairy, the collapsed sheds of the farm,
green-washed walls and bleak, derelict buildings, beams
hanging. There will be sheep-droppings everywhere

in the monastery parlour, where lamps went out long ago
and the warm light fell away, into deep time. The monks,
in brown habits, chanting the *Lumen Christi*, conducted

cosmic stirrings across the island; but theirs was a God
immutable and chastening, their world a garden, fallen
to weed and weevil, because of sin inherited. The parlour,

where whiskey was generously poured, where prayers
were weighty and vows preserved, has long been floorless
and only sheep find shelter against the cloister walls.

*

Turn now, to find the cemetery, with its small
coterie of saints. The plaque says Welcome,
Sister Death. There is peace, and silence, ocean
distantly breathing, breezes sighing absence;

you may find yourself suddenly whelmed
to know how you love this earth, where the Christ
is flesh, and part of it, how people everywhere
are quickening beautiful as light. Radiance comes

from star and planet, the bracing sky is brightening.
Do not say they failed; simply, the precise need
ended. Jesus, awkwardly taken from the cross,

was not a failure. You are on the verge of prayer,
conscious again of our world's grace, aware
of hurrying time, of who you are, and when, and where.

THE FURIES

Amen of the Agony

Atlantic Ocean comes sweeping in
       with violence round the black rocks,
              the waters restive, frantic, passionate;

near shore the 'Great Rock'; further out
       'West Great Rock'; and then – the 'Daisies' –
              submerged, risen, submerged; chaotic with foam

(white, like the flowers) from crashing waves; energy
       of cosmic force, the source that urges
              all creation onwards, outwards, towards

the close, omega, the Pleroma.
       All flesh is flayed by storm, soul is swallowed
              in vastness and spat out; bleak is it, times,

as the sodden yellow-ochre acres of bogland
       eking themselves out from road to distant hills. Then
              the 'dásachtaí', the daisy rocks, the furies –

breaching sometimes, more often known
       only by the feverish whitewaters round them;
              that have drawn currach and trawler to them,

smashed timbers, brasses, iron into sad debris.
　　　Erinyes, the underworld; soul fraught and
　　　　　bewildered, finds yet a still point, Christ-wise,

in the chaos of being; the soothing of spirit,
　　　a white sail distant and holding, islands of the sea
　　　　　glistering in haze on the furthest horizon.

*

From Purteen pier he watched
a tick-tack half-deck trawler slowly
enter the harbour, black smoke roping behind it,
and the cluttered deck dangerous with coil and cord –

back from sea-slaughter, mackerel
cut in half for bait and dumped into a bucket
while up above the seagulls swooped and screamed.
The crew, yellow-bright rubber aprons smeared with blood,

tossing and pitching the catch onto the pier:
blue, the requiem shark, its armoured back, the off-white
flop of its belly, its strike out of darkness, to the kill; conger,
hooped perfection stiffened in the ugliness of death; monkfish,

mud-coloured, freaky, frog-fish and sea-devil,
squatina squatina, sea-bed walker and lurker; splatted
on the pier edge. Fish-boxes, too, sea-flesh, sea-food, ripe.
The vast wreckage of the basking shark, humbled and hauled

up the slipway greased by its blood, to be hacked
and sawn into shivering heaps of blubber. A gentle
monster, jaws gawping open like a barn door. Octopus.
Unlike the watcher, evolution not yet conscious of itself.

*

Behind high walls and a garrisoned gate
full-grown trees, and walking figures, not walking,
merely slow motion, forwards, backwards, willing to meld

with air, to find themselves at rest again,
underground, or tableted to relative oblivion.
Big House hush of grand pianos and black-suited

quartets; no parlour rooms, dim cells only,
with one-way peep-hole, to watch from this world
into a next. Minds strayed, as if out on the bewildering sea,

water-walking over the deeps, the slaughter,
the wrecks, and high above, the stars, rock-dead
in the great vast. Shadows among the olive trees. Demons

cackling in the mind. The pendulum ticks
and tocks, each tick a century, each tock… Like
Ishmael, is he, on the ocean; Yeshua, is he, in the garden;

Legion: floundering among the fluid makings
of the universe. At night sometimes, the inmates
keep a weather eye open, to plead the inscrutable tides

of God, this side of death. Anchored to human
frailty, what can they do but count the bubbles lifting
to the surface and blossoming into air. When we go out

of the demesne of time, this question: what of the broken mind?

*

Light fading; edge of the pounding
Atlantic Ocean; sting of salt on the air; curlews –
challenged congregations scattered
along the shore – lift

strangely musical burble-calls. Herons are mating
high in the canopy of a larch,
shrieking their commitment
to the blessedness of heron, to the gaunt

and elegant ugliness
of their flight. We are, with the crying birds, turf
of the turf, spirit-particle
of the bewildering God. We groan inwardly, leave

illuminated handscripts,
like flowerheads of bog cotton. Picture the man
on his knees in an olive garden;
(the distress oh Christ, my Christ!) cries like notes

played in the high register of the black pianos,
like bird-calls, lapwing, kittiwake. At times the music
seems to be neither of this world
nor the next; there are

silences, attending on the messenger angel. The Word,
taking human flesh out of a too-great love,
found himself ground down
– at the shifting-shingle edge of being –

under the clear incomprehension of his adopted kind
and flung on the shores of suffering.

*

There was a young boy, introvert, involved, grown expert
at the pleasures of isolation, in love with tree-top

and sea-pool, familiar with hawk and yellowhammer,
expert too with the long tapers and Latin responses

– *Kyrie, Requiem, Sanctus* – pattering about the sanctuary
in altar-slippers, preparing for the black-habited and

dismal rituals. Bearing him slowly to consciousness
of human anguish, and of loss. He will ring, as usual,

the bells at sacrament, shut the gilt-bound, delicate pages
of the big book carefully, but tears and keening for the children

burnt to death in Ballymoney will colour the season
sable, will leave his young yet unscathed life exposed, as if

dew-scales had fallen from a perfectly-formed
green leaf and left it bared to a chafing sun.

CARILLON AND BELLS

Amen of Desire

Something stubborn about the call and urge,
how the young man lay in his cramped seminary room
as he watched the progress of the stars across
the night, knowing the world outside is rock

and difficult, sensing the goodness of his body
and its demands, fearing that God was circling him
at a distance like a white-wolf pack at the far
edges of the pines. Soon the bell would ring,

sharply, at the lip of dawn for matins and mental
prayer, with distances ahead for spirit both
and body. Mind, as ever, unquiet, heart swelling

towards a life's willed-for abundance, a love
both delicate and strong, wolf heart, and lamb's,
God longed for, sought through the dark woods.

*

Noontime he had sung, with others,
(like a flock of sea-birds on the shore, facing
into the winds) Palestrina: *sicut cervus desiderat*...Mid-

afternoon, in the conservatory – a great, inverted
glass bowl, with beams of cedar, with bougainvillea,
the Silk Road giant lily – the words and music haunted,

'like the deer my soul thirsts for you, oh Lord', as if it were
the Magdalen, tip-toeing towards the tomb. *Sehnsucht*;
yearning, *desiderium*... Dressed in black soutane and cincture

and still young, question of will, and constancy,
question, too, of profound reservations. Late afternoon
he climbed to the dusty music-room in the seminary attic

to practise on the old upright piano: Liszt's
Liebestraum, but it was all false notes and butter-fingers,
all inconsistency. Late evening, the sky was a rich patterning

of saffron light and a full moon lounged at rest
behind threads of cloud, while the incomprehensible
heavens were punctured by faint stars. The city skyline fell away

in darkness; he watched that foresting of lights,
and thought of all who would lie, like him, that night,
unquiet, the ache in the heart uneased, the thirst unquenched.

*

Under the dust-heavy alders and the briars, here
where the city trams go past with a great hiss,
tilts a small, half-hidden one-person tent, dark blue,
with trash and cans around, a foetid smell, a nobody

living rough. Not far the ever-present invitation
of the canal. One God-chastened, God-cherished
soul has come to this. Late-day winds are ferrying
rain across the trees; traffic wheezes, urgent for home,

carrying through the city the vehemence of a new
millennium. Faint light appears, sickly, through
the plastic of the tent. Perhaps here the Christ
will dine tonight, or call a friend to him in the hours

before dawn. Earth spins; here is a soul flung
into elliptical orbit around the sun, human mechanisms
coming undone at the welds, the rivets, the soldering;
as if God Yahweh had drifted out into darkspace.

*

I was driving home when I spotted it: the snipe –
bog-bleater, she-goat of the air –
this small-bang explosion
out of the aftergrass that will rocket away,
low over the wetlands and the bottoms, that
disappears through a hole in the glowering sky,

now caught, this winter dusk, in the car's headlights,
so out-of-place and present it shocked
and delighted, this old evolution's
almost-perfect bird-body,
this mistress of flight, this
querulous miracle of the countryside.
Comes, I thought, from somewhere
beyond the ditch, some local, cosmic source, hides
over the rainbow, beyond human fumbling.

*

Snow has been falling through the darkness,
the night sky blotted out, with its innumerable

stars and galaxies; tomorrow
the fields and hedgerows will be lit

by a generous blanketing of white. Annual
the marvel of it, the shortwhile

loveliness and wonder. Even more wonderful
the miracle: that already

before the Word that set the marvel of creation
in evolving motion – over 13 billion years, imagine! –

you and I, in our souls and bodies, were destined
to be together in the miracle of love, for this

short, this irreplaceable, lifetime. We, as one,
being more than selves, we are earthed, part

of the full moon risen high over the red gate, part
of the young hare, unafraid, settled

among the fading rudbeckia, sharing
these years, the darkness and light, the grief, the gladness.

for Ursula

*

It was a long day of spittling rain; the ugly
old-brown walls of the hospital
appeared to sweat; a little chatter in the corridors,
the waiting-rooms crowded, one small boy irritatingly

tock-tocked his foot against a chair-leg. A neon light,
on in the grey-bleak afternoon, was flickering; couples
sitting apart together, murmuring, watching the clock.
I whispered to myself: Oh Christ, my Christ.

But we were given glimpses into the being of cosmos –
the sonogram: black and white and greyscale,
placenta, the baby – the amniotic sea, the spirit
moving over the waters, offending chaos; it was

a shumbling vision, beautiful and awful, the heartbeat,
chest, neck, the umbilical cord… moment to cherish,
to hold faith, bells ringing deep in the heart, carillon, love;
and the decisions, there since the Big Bang, locus earth,

place Dublin, time the twenty-first century, year of the Lord.
I prayed to honour them, the ancestors in their pale awayness,
and our own impatiently waiting generations. A hint
of a soft-flesh, soft-bone, stirring contradiction

to nihilism, like Vincent's painting of *Almost Blossom* in San Rémy,
or Czeslaw Milosz's 'one real droplet of dew'. This day
we coasted with the guiding angels, with saints and birdsong
of galaxy and star. I whispered to myself: Oh Christ, my Christ.

THE HOME PLACE

Amen of Birdsong, of the Saints and Angels

Cattistock, in Dorset; go through the kissing-gate and make your way onto the public footpath; there will be sheep and you will feel for them, their matter, the hard bone of their hooves, the stone that is stuff of their brains.

Through the next iron gate, its high squeal, low groan, and in the wet hollow between trees the holy well, in dark shadow, trickles slowly, its waters disappearing in source and destination.

A robin, solitary, watches you from the alders, its song as old as psalm and chronicle.

Twilight is grey, slightly misty.

The churchyard with its leaning bockety gravestones holds its humps of grass in quietness; the church itself, stout in buttress and stone-angled presence,

stands doleful, watchword and reassurance.

There is a wooden gate into the village; the latch sticks a little; the one long street is deserted under off-yellow light.

Hesitantly you enter the 'Fox and Hounds'; all heads turn, in sudden silence, until you find a corner, under black beams, sit in relief and wait. Here you would draw a curtain against all difference, remembering that solitary boy who knelt, years gone, on a window-seat, face against cold glass, gazing out onto improbable imaginings.

What purpose the unweaving and unravelling, if not for the sake of marvel, what purpose the searching all without, since you hold within you the Christ, closer to you than the stirrings of your heart?

Now you share with the one you love a sweet Dorset cider, with hill lamb and champ and Dorset apple cake.

You are content.

Too soon it is dark outside, time to amble back.

There is rain, a soft wind bustling wet against you, together you are hastening

back through the churchyard and along the path; a sheep, eyes wide with fright, leaps away from human presence into the thickening night.

*

Saints and angels, of all feathers, pass at will
between time and timelessness; like birds, they
have their languages and only God can comprehend them all;

the words I write – although recalcitrant –
come shyly out of multitudes, they seek to clarify, and they
– in their unruly way – attempt to prophesy, for they are placed

between there and here, between then
and now, to signify the end-in-view, Omega, the Christ.
Birdsong and birds, the choiring of saints and angels, rehearse

that purity I strain for, as Messaien worked
to vocalise the blackbirds, larks and nightingales, the sounds
he discovered in the veins of the meadows, in the forest's bones –

bird-notes, marshland chords, calls, trills, croaks,
the hard-ground treading of saints and the Ariel hastening
of angels, though, having suffered the tuneless hearts of Nazi camps

he knew that even the most tender music breasts
against the edging of death, and therefore translated his songs
into the hammers, wires and ivories of two raven-black grand pianos.

*

The past is a scattering of barnacled rocks
        at the edge of ocean; indoors we keep
journals of sorrows and accidents, though
        most wonderful has been the ongoing
common everyday, too easily forgotten:
        letters cut into the gravestone, merge
with the stone. Back door, its ditch-dark green,
        rain-swollen, scraping open or scraping shut
has scored a perfectly-shaped quarter-circle
        on the black flags and gouged a large splinter
out of itself at the base where a field-mouse
        might whisper through. One nightfall, Christmas
Eve – before electricity had driven angels and all
        supernaturals off the island, when oil-lamps
still stood elegant, like women in a painting
        by Toulouse-Lautrec – father took me out
into the heathlands, the hill lit only by a weak
        starlight; then turned me round to see:
in all the windows of the houses, there were
        candles lighting, their intimacy and presence

transfiguring the world. I stood, awed and,
      somehow, triumphant. No lights have ever since

been adequate, to the birth, to the remembrance.

*

[from 'A Leitrim Townland', by Ursula Foran: Leitrim Guardian, 2018]

    'It is hard to imagine that, before the ravaging of their potato crop,
    upwards of seventy people lived here. It is also hard to imagine that,
    even further back, these fields and rocks echoed to the tones of the
    Irish language for far longer than to the English we now speak here.'

These are the fields of Leitrim, and here
the wild meadow, grasses, with celandine, meadowsweet
and maidenhair…
Apple trees down by the red gate, a chestnut tree

from Herbert's Leighton Bromswold, an oak –
thriving – from an acorn Heaney gathered by Thoreau's
Walden Pond.
In the wet-daub earth is the dwelling-place of our unruly God;

birdsong perfected, even jackdaw, heron, water-hen,
the very shrieks of hooded crow and magpie, those street-cleaners
and working angels
of an evolving world. Ancestors, in the lenient light of eternity,

hover here; wonder holds itself against us, for we are
finite insects grasping for infinity. It is cosmos, the spirit
coming down like dewfall,
and onerous our tasks of care. Soon the wild meadow

will renew itself, in season, accommodating deaths
and rebirths; familiar world, beautifully unfamiliar, enriched,
enriching,
with, sometimes, the scarlet call of a poppy.

*

The portal through which you have entered this world
is not the one through which you will exit. In Bunnacurry,

gravemounds shuffle over against one another
while ghostly mists relentlessly pass across, water dreeps

from stone crosses, from fuchsia where robin and wren
fall silent; a heron stands firm as an effigy near a ditch;

even the keeper of the graves has gone to ground,
the rusting gate has a rusting lock. Grandfather lies

in a grave too large for him, saxifrage and lungwort
cover him, and small white-stone chippings. This world

enclosed, is a garden, perishable and bewildering; holds
the quiet of a Vermeer interior, the sure-footed steps

of a Bach partita. What is it, then, that has flung you
off your horse into the dust and blinded you with light?

Gather yourself off the ground; there is one who is; seek
him out, present yourself at his door; he asks only your love.

*

He who sets the aurora in the clouds is enamoured
of human, earth and cosmos; for what would he be

without song-birds? without saints and angels?

enamoured, too, of the billions of insects daily sucked
into the radiators of long-distance trucks come crossing
the careening world: signals of the broken Christ;

(and where have they taken him, my courteous Lord?)
There is, too, the improbable colouring of parakeets,
the notion of time, the imponderable size of the universe.

Unbelievable the human spine with its curves and vertebrae
in under the skin as Himalayas and Karakorum are snuggled
in under snow; and the rainbow, its spectrum, stretching

from heart to heart, from Achill Island to the Antarctic.
It is heavy-duty soil out there, beyond and beyond, with
lavish mansions of the blessed dead; the children of light –

guiding angels of the galaxies – are shoaling in their billions
beyond our ken, the first frontier being flesh, the second,
clay. I am in body, bodily, on this island, earthed. I know

the world to be a living thing, a heart beating in every tree,
everything in motion, call it love, the agape of rock
and marigold, and the eros of a selfless sympathy.

*

I came back to my place in the pew, self-conscious
as always, and knelt to savour, as always,

the bread, unleavened. Hard November sunlight
scarce touched the early chill, and the windows

were colouring the day: emerald, blood-red
and Virgin blue. I could sense around me

the earthly living, and at my back the dead; waves
of refugees fell and rose within me, the children,

orphaned and at sea. It was a hosting, then and there,
heart calling to heart, squalls across the galaxies,

the chalice, embossed and silver-wrought, lifted
into the air in spate. I could hear, for a moment,

the music of oneness, and like Beethoven's 9th
creation played its symphony with all the instruments

and the cosmic voices in full harmony. I bowed my head
and closed my eyes. And then there were only –

candles lit before the November list of names
of the dead, the sounds of a small-town congregation

shuffling back to the pews, and clouds outside
bringing the chancel back, as always, into gloom.

POINT OF PURE TRUTH

Amen of Judgement

Around the baptismal font, *point vierge*, back
of the church, they are standing – grandfather,
still sprightly, grandmother, not yet slowed in flesh;
their daughter, weak after the birthing, but radiant;

son-in-law, upright and brimming-over father;
godmother, early twenties, tuberculosis; godfather,
wooing her in hopelessness; the baby, unaware
and snuffling; the celebrant, with the oils and words.

A moment merely, out of the incomprehensible
immensity that is time; all of them decades dead,
save the baby, who is stooped now with age, where I

stand again, by the font; it is still that moment, they are
all there, attendant, as they were, and will be. Point
vierge. The spirit still moving over the waters.

*

I have sought a living poetry, written out of spirit
in the on-going love-affair between self and world,
to yield a deepening understanding and a widening

tenderness, that will save us from the hell of remorseless
logic, from transhumanism and artificial intelligence;
a poetry of verve and muscle, with insinuating music, no

versification for corners of the comics page; a poetry
of soul's integrity and venture. I would have words
of prophecy, holding the door ajar between past and now,

now and future, words to touch the heart of star
and starfish, of ancient lands where the people, in our time,
have been marshalled into darkness. The big book tells

how the Lord called Samuel the third time; he arose and went
to Eli and said, *Here I am, you called me.* And Eli knew it was
the Lord who called, and Eli said to Samuel: *Go, lie down;*

*if you hear the call again you will say: Speak, Lord, your servant
is listening.* I seek a garnering of words that touch beyond
the trite, towards transcendence, words laboured for and gifted,

so now I try for silence and sitting still, attendant on the spirit,
I question what I have come to, why so much time has been
allotted to me. I have attempted to play a plausible music,

beyond processes of was, and is, and will-be. Someday
there will be the final lines, last words will have been set down,
completed, and incomplete. Poems, like sycamore seeds, will be

free to wander in whatever breeze will take them, carrying
their burdens. I will have prayed: Spare me Lord for my days
burn off like dew, place, oh Christ, your angels as a fence about me.

*

The river was beautiful, dark water running smoothly before the rocks,
silver-white and golden-ochre as it broke; below the rocks the pool, calm
as if in world-satisfaction, promise in its depths.

Father fishing; absorbed in the world.

When he had the trout up on the bank, the sorrow began within me;
that innocent lithe body, its gold-brown colouring, spots on its skin like
miniature haloes; eye wide, unmoving, lips hard, mouth gasping.

Father put his thumb inside, forced back the head and I heard bones
snapping. I almost wept; but this was my father fishing, who was spring
and flow for me; he was absorbed, then, in the world but I felt something
in creation's plan move towards disorder.

When the quintet stepped out onto the stage, I was sad, too; they were elderly, white-haired, fumbly, the door banged back behind them as they foostered towards the chairs, while I became aware of the hard bench under me.

Three old gentlemen; one old woman, a younger one at the piano.

They sat, ordering themselves to a settling of instruments, bows and strings, the piano stool, the tautness of the instruments like the stiffness of the flesh.

I was dismayed. Schubert: Die Forelle. Then

they began. Within moments, it was father again, absorbed in the world; there was an early summer breeze, the sun shone; stream-water sparkled, fitting itself wholly into itself; earth a joy, azure the unattainable sky; piano runs and playfulness, strings like lithe bodies in fluid mastery.

When I opened my eyes I saw them, the elders, flux and energy of their bodies absorbed from one another, moving like reed-beds, like water-lilies and it was love, it was the spirit breathing again through Genesis, as if the seniors were extracting order and not imposing it; disparate they were, shifting in their own breezes, yet shifting as one, their parts moving, the whole refigured, segment and whole resolving.

I found myself, afterwards, exhausted, laid out on the green fields of the world, hurt, and never so alive.

*

There was a storm, withering through the trees.
I was safe in the drawing-room. I had been
tinkering a little on the piano, had played
poorly. Frustrated again, I took up the poem;

waited. There was no stir. I must have dozed,
for it was surely dream that came to me. There were
three, like the staid and fetching angels who appeared
out of the desert before the tent of Abraham.

We sat, for a time and out of time; they asked,
without speaking. *I believe*, I answered, also
without speaking: *I believe I had said yes; I certify to this:*
that God is true. They said they had come to ring

the bells of evidence. I pleaded – no: I had not yet
credited the poem I was to write. Silence again.
I heard a small bell tinkling, like the bells of
Elevation. I whispered to them again – *No, I have not*

been proved worthy; and what, I asked, *what*
of the lover, Crucified? So: silence a while, for a time
and out of time. Till they seemed to fade, like dew
from leaves of the thorn-bush. I thought

I heard a bell toll somewhere in the distance.
I woke; the Angelus bell was sounding from
the monastery. There were three guttering candles
with wax starting to spill over on the piano lid.

*

I have turned a corner and find that I am old,
the language of my body is stuttering and slow;
                             age, like a mist,
has come upon me by surprise;

I have turned a corner and find that I am one
of a diminished generation, challenging old dogma –
                             but who have held firm
to the goal, the Omega, the Christ.

Today I watched an old, slowed ram, black-face,
wool shabby and tacked with clay, taking his ease
                            in the wet wild meadow
and gazing at his ewes from a distance; he was feeding

on bitter windfall apples in the sweetest aftergrass, a ram
not remorseful for his vanities, nor for the wicked
                            hard-bone spirals
of his horns. Now I find that the body,

in its mellow shrivelling, is nothing beautiful;
night-time, the eyes are more often open
                            on the slow-waltz
movements of star and planet. Night-time I hold

it is not necessary to kneel in judgement on the self,
to the Christ desire alone will be eloquent.
                            Now I sit, content,
on the canal-bank bench, watching the swans

worry at their feathers, white down gathering in beautiful
disorder, where I can honour the elderly-gentleman
                            elegance on the water,
the handsome dowager waddling across the grass.

LIKE THE DEWFALL

Amen of the Consummation

I stood, smitten and tongue-tied, and held the latch lest it slam
the thick paint-blistered door
between the dim-lit kitchen and the free yard outside
where green slime trailed down

the side of the water-butt. Maggie, too old, still young,
was bent double with arthritis;
she ushered me, kindly, in. The kitchen was time and place
of poverty and unwitting graciousness,

odour of age, of damp, of stone floors; you, too, oh Christ,
my Christ, were there, becurled and
ineffective, boasting, centre-chest, a heart on fire: presiding
over a damp-turf smoke-chocked fire.

Maggie, under her burden of skirts and woollens, sent me
down to the lower room to greet
her whine-voiced mother; in that cavern-dark space there was a reek
of blankets, urine, counterpanes,

the ancient woman dim and frightening, almost animal
in her stare and breathing;
I, child I, did not understand; it was an ending, slow and ugly,
an untriumphant eking-away of living;

she muttered something spittly at me, I nodded, turned, and
when I came back, Maggie
had wrapped the eggs in pages of 'Ireland's Own'. At last, to hear
the click of the latch behind me

was relief beyond relief. But your words echo still within me:
'blessed are you poor', and 'come to me,
ye burdened'. Now it is you, Oh Christ, my Christ, are begging,
you who are dying for my love.

*

At the bedrock of the cross I stand appalled;
at times I see you, Christ, barefoot by the lake,

praying; crowds crush forward, you – who have been
watching out over the water – turn to them,

heroic and alone. You have come upon me,
over decades, entering my heart, stealthily,

like the dewfall. Slaughters, disasters, assaults
burst in on our TV; the authorities,

upright folk, wring the usual words, presenting
vinegar. Nevertheless: *Haec nox est*, we will sing,

lest we forget. My words, of praise and pleading
– astonished still by your fierce, unmeasured love,

offered against despair and nothingness – fall
like stones, like teardrops, beneath your hurting feet.

*

A storm was crowding in off the Atlantic,
bringing darkness, rain
and sudden squalls; I sheltered in Bunnacurry church,
reading Isaiah: *'many were appalled at him ;*

like one from whom the people hide their faces, he was
despised, and we held him
in low esteem'. I looked up at the crucifix
over the altar; it was of silver and bronze, artfully wrought.

An old man was shuffling around the stations,
faded brown jacket, baggy
corduroys, mouthing the words in a muffled whisper;
old islandman, I thought, old faith. The winds cried, rains

spattered the windows. I closed my eyes awhile, wearied,
till I felt a hand touch me
on the shoulder; a man, of uncertain age, but old,
stood over me; he wore a robe of rough material, dark-wood

brown, brown leather belt, a long beard of purest white, white
hair, somewhat unkempt, to his shoulders.
It was the eyes, a light and piercing blue, that burned through
into my soul. 'You have stolen up on me,' I said,

'like a revenant.' He smiled, then turned his gaze
to the crucifix, shivered a little. I suspected drink…
'That is not how it was,' he whispered, pointing;
'not stylized, no comfort, no repose; can one go so deep

into the abyss, unshuddering?' He stood above me; 'Who
are you?' I asked him. 'I was,' he said,
'John, brother to James, the sons of Zebedee. Sons
of Thunder,' and he laughed, quietly. 'I laid,' he said,

'my head against his breast and knew that strong heart
beating, heart of the cosmos,
of the earth and heavens, source where love and life
are rooted. By night they dragged him, tortured, mocked him,

and around noon they crucified him outside the city wall.
I watched the one who is
source and sustenance, goal of a living universe
suffer more than any human ever ought to know; he writhed

against the timber, I could count his bones, I could not
turn away; a ragged loin-cloth was heavy
with his blood. Oh my Yeshua!' he sighed,
'you took upon yourself all knowledge of human suffering.'

He paused, he took my right hand in a fierce grip, I could feel
the bones, and drew away from him, quickly. 'We
took him down, rested the broken body on Miriam's lap. I
laid my head against his bloodied chest and that strong heart

had ceased to beat. The sky had turned black, the clay
trembled; I was certain
our world had ended.' He sighed and fell silent a while. 'But
we met again! in dawnlight, by the lakeshore, on his journey

back from the tomb. One more time I leant against his breast, knew
the strong and eternal beating
of his heart.' He smiled at me, sighed again: 'I was tasked,'
he said, 'to live, unlike the others; tasked with words, to tell

of love, forgiveness, of the thrust of all creation's growth
towards that great heart.'
'How,' I asked him then, 'how can I sing the Lord's song
in a dead land?' (Those piercing eyes!) 'Trust,' he said, 'your voice,

your words. He is word. Speak him.' I lowered my head,
closed my eyes, a moment, merely. Shaken.
When I looked up he was gone. There was only the old man
of the stations, lighting candles before the shrine of Mary.

*

In the nuns' garden the sisters stand apart, shy birds
on the shore of a pounding sea. I am awed
by the tongue's fidelity to silence, by the will's

self-confining strength in a bare cell. I had thought of them
as dead before they are dead. In the ordered graveyard
small iron crosses stand in their neat rows, names in faith,

dates of birth and death; over them all the delicate,
persistent blossoms of the saxifrage. I saw, in fissures
of sunlight, blue-glossed ravens exulting on the air;

there were scents of oleander, of thyme, of extravagant
heathers; I looked for the stillness of the high, white lily.
Beyond the walls, each day brings us reading in the papers

of yesterday's death routines. *Ein jeder Engel*, I remembered,
ist schrecklich; and do the angels fly, I wondered, late and late,
across the black night sky, to roost? The big book tells

that even the unproductive sand, the marram, the sand-eel,
will flush, after all, into the joy of the festive song of songs
across all the unthinkable, all-sainted, infinite demesnes of God.

*

Day dying in the outer suburbs; a quiet,
settling. Unfussed, relishing – alongside

the woman he loves – boxty potato pancakes
with parsley butter melting over; shrimp,

in garlic and lemon, sizzling on the skillet;
a pinot grigio, that honeysuckle flavour…

Then stands outside in the warm dusk, faint
sounds of distant traffic, scarcely a zephyr-breath

touching the high ash-trees; the soft shudder
of a boiler coming to life. Earlier he had walked

where mallard and water-hen had been busy
about their mating rituals, their rushes and flurries

across the waters of the canal, stirred by original
freshness and urgency. He inhaled, luxuriously; knew

that the people whom he loved were here, revelling,
everywhere around, and waiting. Night closing in;

soon, raspberry and rhubarb crumble, with a small
dollop of cream; a film, perhaps, on the TV;

anticipating always the savoury heaviness of sleep.
Brittle-hipped, a little arthritic and taut of hearing,

climbing contentedly, but cautiously, upstairs.
Amen, he says, Amen; oh Christ, my Christ, Amen

Note: The writing of poems may sometimes need to be postponed, by pausing and taking stock, or being brought to a halt by insight, accident or prophecy. Such work may easily be termed 'stations of the soul', the hiatus in the on-going movement of creation around the writer bringing words to bear on the moment or moments before stepping back again and continuing with the journey. The present gathering of such works, though appearing now, were stations met and passed over the last number of years. Putting them together may shape part of a life, a section of the journey I have been on between birth and death, between early January of any one year and late December of any later year. Many of these pieces began as work towards poems and ended up as 'prose-poems'; the others insisted on making runs and rushes towards the sonnet structure without broaching the traditional form, but approaching it, poems that see themselves as part of a sequence as a whole, and not as individual pieces independently complete.

NEW POEMS: FOR THE TIMES AND SEASONS

1. NOTES FROM THE OUTER SUBURBS

There are cats erwauling from one high hedge to another
in off-lemon moon-misted light from the tall streetlamps;

there is stench of feral catpiss in the suburbs, cats
multiplying in the briar growths of back gardens. Woodlice

winter in the ash-wood logs, scattering to escape
a suddenly disruptive light when the log-pile shifts.

Rarely now, the council trucks come hosing down
the street-kerb gutters. In easterly gales the iron door

– rusted round its edges – into the scrap back garden,
bangs at irregular intervals, loose-locked. The world

grows old in shards and snatches; we, temporary beings,
are moths in erratic flight between one seed-head

and another, though at times we may be butterflies,
wings against the sun alight like stained-glass windows.

*

First snowdrops show like flakes left by a white winter;
pavements are stained after the ruck and rot of leaves;

day starts with the fresh breath of a lemon-grey sunlight,
the gleam and turning of cars, out from constricted driveways.

There is a bronze sheen on the variegated ivy, the burgeoning
of potted pansy and geranium, sour-milk blossoms of magnolia.

In the city park, mute swans thrash and wing-flap, the cob
riding the pen almost to drowning, crushing her as he beaks her neck

and lowered head; he finishes, and turns away, indifferent.
I have been seeking another name for 'God': the names I know

grow stale. I search the novelties of the new estates, Mercedes,
Lexus, BMW; houses on view, the mortgages. The heavyweight

heirloom of the Old Testament is stored above stairs, now
new gangs come, fishing through the letterbox for our car keys.

*

Noon-time across the suburbs. No bell rings. Lilac
flourishes, there is rich flowering on the chestnut trees.

With bills and invitations the postman has passed by.
On red-tiled roofs, magpies chatter from the chimney-pots;

the trees breathe health and light, the dogwood flush. Moths,
grey-white, white-blue, are hesitant between poppy-heads

and the light on the back porch; we stand, watching,
a basin, maybe, in our hands, peels, a squeezed-out

lemon; or a bottle of chilled white wine, réserve, two
glasses. *Libera nos*, we whisper: deliver us from evil.

The love that held us strong over the dark centuries, seems
to have been lost in this, the brightest; the younger generations

so furiously rage together, like Vikings newly-minted, don't hear
the gossiping flock of whooper swans fly over, don't

raise their eyes to the thousand starlings in dark ballet
of swirling flight through a dusky mid-summer eve.

Clouds pewter-dark by afternoon; dogs are being walked
through the estates, with excited yappings – sometimes at night

you hear them mourn for the days of savagery when dog
fought dog and revelled in the blood-lust of beasthood, high

howling against the moon. We, unsettled in our sleep,
moan and shift in bed, half-chilled. By morning, small dogs

are being walked again through the estates, corseted
in pinafore and plaid coats, basket cases, and beribboned.

The ice-cream van, its tinkle-tickle call, passes noisily
down the cul-de-sac; the patrol car, too, comes prowling,

waits, its engine ticking. In the corner of the living-room,
the outdoors is a fish-tank with its bubbles, guppies, angels.

*

Do not mock it, this is our life, where we work at importunate
stirrings of the spirit. At odd times the Christ – ascetic, cynical –

tramps round the old estates, offering leaflets, *no junk please*,
upsetting phone-watch, alarm systems; at times the jagged edge

of his thumbnail scrapes against the ribs. Though he is the zee,
the omega of all desire, the mind is cluttered with the residues

of the frustrating years. In the dark of night, every beating heart
lies open. In the new estates: Cedar, Yew-Tree, Oak, no hearse

has yet made entrance; but there have been night ambulances,
neighbours at their windows, watching. *A thaisce*! treasure! listen!

in the deep heart's caverns, amidst ruckus of this day's business,
be a Bethany to him, steal to him in the darkest angles of night;

when angers threaten the city, his care persists, holds you in his love's
abundance, Christ shuffling through the debris of the old estates.

2. FOR THE TIMES AND SEASONS

The Parachute

We wake up in this world, mornings, and ache
because we are incomplete; there is rain, the day

will be written grey. What I garner may be negligible,
even so I will give thanks. Earth, too, aches, straining,

brings, in Wales, a school-house down on the children;
in Haiti she rouses ocean to flood the shabbier streets

to ruin. One peace-filled evening I watched a fawn, vigilant
under the faint light of stars; I sensed us both together

precious. We know grief grew from the soil in the beginning
and has not yet been rooted out; the fog of our unseeing

has been lifting slowly, allowing little sunlight through. Once
I stood in a field in France, in the warm dusk, and heard

a parachute frrip-frrap open somewhere high above and knew,
gratefully, that the human heart is, at its best, indomitable.

Mind, mornings, may be scraggy as the heron's nest high in the ruffled treetops;

the child in me wants to be an old-time cowboy riding a palomino across the high sierras, inhaling orange dust, while vultures wheel in the air above,

wants to be the suave and grease-haired still-young and not-yet-disillusioned toreador sipping chilled Marqués de Cáceres rosé wine on a Toledo terrace.

That same child went slithering on the earth, felt himself the spirit's whipping-boy, imposed upon by the angels and the beasts, knew in flesh and bones the draw of flight, while loving the moss beneath his naked feet and pining to master thermals above the clouds;

but still he is holding

belief in sunlight, in white sheets strung along blue skipping-rope and hoisted high into sea-shore winds, remembering – spite of falls and knee-cuts – the small boy's small-flowered wellingtons asplash on the sky that found itself mirrored in a snow-melt pool.

A BOYCHILD
for Thomas Leonard

Canal water is fugged with trash and trailing weeds,
water-striders perform Waldteufel's *Skaters' Waltz*

on the wrinkled surfaces; after the rush of it crashing down
into the lock, the water drags its way through the suburbs

like an overgrown laneway down to an abandoned farm;
small boys, all dressed in off-black, fish under the bridge,

a scattering of stiffened maggots lying at their feet; small
bream and roach, tiddlers and tittlebats, with hints of bronze,

lie stunned a while in big jam-jars before they are flung back
into their element. Baby sleeps in the new pram, while ambulance

police and firemen go screaming by. I would will him to be
non-acquiescent to a callous age, that his gentleness

may become a byword hereabouts. Peace, I pray, to surpass
all understanding, be his, and a cherishing of all the little ones.

*   *   *

On the split lip of the cliff I watched a tiny spittle of clay, merest trickle – in
the wind's breath – down the rock face.

A cold spring moon, in daylight, hung like a disc of silk, transparent, over
the ruined houses at the sea's edge.

Inishmurray. Abandoned island, old as chaos.

Here, centuries ago, ascetics whipped themselves towards obedience, and in more recent Ireland a bent-near-double father carried from here his daughter's rope-tied suitcase down to the emigrant boat – one day of sunshine, lark song vibrant in the air;

now I, gripping the roots of heather for hold, lift myself to the stratified island, to find a foothold in the flux.

*　*　*

You may hear the whistle-song of the entropy-bird in the wet spruce-log burning in the stove, watch the slight flame of the primrose-candle, secret in the mesh of a scarified ditch;

the one, like prayer, rooted to the sky, and one – like faith – with roots in the living soil:

earth humming everywhere, the white blossoms of the blackthorn stirring in their opulence, the sudden birds – robin, tit and wren – hastening to courtship and nesting.

And I am greedy now of time, knowing the past – because it is – with both a sad and a glad, clarity: ash, blackened wick, and smoke; it is not yet clear if there will be some fruitfulness, a something else I cannot name; just as – when the store was burned down that night in Bunnacurry and I stood with other children, awed – I watched in silence old men scurrying, bewildered, backlit shadows against the flames.

*　*　*

Mid-morning quiet in the townland; the postman has gone, glissando, by; delivery trucks have been and even the lapdogs who fancied themselves as wolverines a while, have fallen still.

I have settled in a patch of meadow, to pray in a rustle of longing towards my God but winds of the world come whistling through, and the myriads of branches in my mind's deep woods hustle noisily.

I know how my Christ stays watchful as a fox, biding time; how love will touch each falling raindrop, each circling satellite, each far-out hurtling galaxy, every crash and ping of the cosmos – while I circle that still and clamouring point from which all things take being;

but, like Job, like Job I have made covenant with him, he will know my ways, will number all my veins, will harvest my desires.

The ocean rumbles nearby; the sand-grains shift and fall.

* * *

I can dream in the presence of hollyhock and delphinium, of soft-pink rose and lupin where bumble-bee and variegated Eden-coloured butterflies speak ease and silence and the passion of earthly things.

Otherwise belief, with its creel of prayer and ritual and mystery, becomes difficult.

All winter they brought their dead to the ports and gates, and while we live their shades will haunt our being.

And though we colour the walls with the figures of dread: dragons and demons, with the cockerel betrayal of the Christ, there is still barbarian terror abroad, innocence of bird and tree and the vituperative slinking of cat.

Astrantia, Fuchsia, Poppy, Rose, these are our prayers, too, they are hallowing our days.

We offer our hymns to the vesper candle-flame and sink into moth-silent night.

* * *

On a bright March morning, the long-tailed tits were gathering on the old hawthorn tree in a blur of black and white and pink, chasing and cavorting, a rare frenzy of activity in the monastery garden.

Playful shouts drifted from a nearby schoolyard, shrieks of delight mingling with the delicate bird calls.

An elderly nun approached along the path in slow, arthritic steps carefully placed; she leaned heavily on her walking frame, head bowed with the weight of decades, sky-blue rosary beads slipping through her fingers: … *for us sinners, now and at the hour…*

By the hawthorn tree, something caught her attention; fingers gnarled as twigs of the tree, she gripped tightly on the frame, slowly raised her head.

Rosary and arthritic pain forgotten she watched the birds in their energetic dance: …*as it was in the beginning, is now…*

In a few weeks' time, she knew, the bare hawthorn would exult in the whitest blossoms; she, too, would blossom, soon, perhaps too soon, and be filled with playfulness like the school-children, would fly free like the long-tailed tits.

SOMETHING

At the edge of understanding there is something that is not
some thing; blink, one mild dusk, then open your eyes to glimpse

shadow-forms by the red gate that disappear at once – blink
again, and others… and disappear… and…

something to be grasped; a meaning, perhaps everything, perhaps
someone; a purpose in the whirlpool of midges through the moist air

and in the gold-paint glow in the topmost shiver-leaves of the ash,
intuited before glimpsed, that near-thing that almost was,

touching some inner chord of the heart, a moment scarcely,
exotic though undiscovered, in the midst of the most dull

and unimportant chores, an existence between the i and s of is;
the bliss of almost-intoxication in self-conscious sobriety,

our living, skipped a moment into spirit, out again, a tease
and beckoning, a test of alpha-omega, of language and of being.

* * *

Sometimes you, my Christ, are lake-water lilies, yellow-gold, purple heart at ease amongst upholding sweet-green leaves, and then I see my life, bounded by bogland and bogland fragrances, trailing like water-weed, in a green uselessness.

You remind me – bog-pools are treacherous, oozing bubbles, to drown the unwary, the soft-shoe-soled heart; but then there is the arum lily, in the shed, in a neglected pot amongst paint-tins and muck-hardened gloves where you – after a drought of forty days or so – blossomed unasked, great blood-red petals opening like a wound, on a long bean-like stem where you waited, eager for me, but reaching out for care.

* * *

In stained-wood pews, I was cassocked in darkness, surpliced in light;

I turned to face what is airy, trusting in it, and turned back, in confusion, to what is earthen, its delighting eccentricities, mind and heart not yet sufficiently aligned.

In Lenten liturgy, two small blocks of wood clattered together instead of the gently tinkling bells that told us the Lord was amongst us in white-coated sacrament.

In prescribed texts, the constancy, the polyphonies – I was held safe in spite of infidelities and under-the-skin imperfections – world like the glass snow-globe that – when you turned it upside-down – sent peach-blossoms floating in dream-space.

* * *

High in the angle of the doorway, small as a tennis ball, this wasps' nest, too, is in itself a universe, with working lives and constancy, where the angels ascend, descend on dewfall ladders, where the stalwart creatures, dreaded and despised, have their own exits and their entrances, where Mars, in its returns, sheds fizzy-orange-coloured honey light across the nebulae;

there is a season, there is the queen and foundress, and there are the wasps, yellowjackets, that hold in their bodies the memory of earth when the forests did not echo with the shouts of men, that build nests of tissue-paper chewed from wood and stuck together with saliva;

born to it, with venom and barbed sting merely for self-protection, they weave a zig-zag path through air leading unerringly to their miracle-home, wasp nest a wonder fistful of being and I hold no authority to cast it down: for we know unless the Lord helps build the city, they labour in vain who build it.

GREYLAG

Over the suburbs two great flocks of greylag
flew low out of the evening;

from ragged chevron shapes, their bleak contralto calling
faded and fell to silence inside the dusk;

they brought with them the chill of marshlands
and the shivering reed-notes of an alien music;

a grey-toothed haw already lay on the car roof
and though the soul

hefted itself a little to the unexpected and the mystery,
the turning of the season was a long way off;

there was stillness, save for the evening traffic's
wearying noises, faint from the road,

and the pulsing life-breath of the Proud Unfolding Spirit,
bearing the straining breasts and wings of the wild geese.

* * *

Holy Saturday: always, a fire of broken timbers lit in a rickety brazier, men standing around, a little embarrassed, in the thickening dusk; later, moonlight will show the town below darkened and darkening, like a still from an old movie.

Fire, filched from the brazier, lights a candle carried into the church, startling darkness;

a dribble of light-hot-grease falls on my wrist from the small candle I hold;

there is agreeable chinking of the censer chains, the seeds of incense smoking, exotic scent, acceptable.

The light and fire, here contained, spell out an inarticulate yearning, to hold this *ignis fatuus*, this Vulcan faith, this unbelievable belief, in an unwavering grasp.

We stand. We kneel. Prayers lift like smoke. Tomorrow the ashes will be scattered out over the hungry grass.

* * *

Around the Mall in Westport and over the dark on-flowing of the river, you will see them, like black chestnuts, clumped nightshade or death's head on the high wind-shaken braches, the crows – rook and carrion, hooded monk and clown jackdaw, their black masses, their raucous sermonising one to another in caw-words, unmusical, echoing, in their own church, structured and unreasoning, hallowed between street and sky, above roof and scuttling umbrellas, bustleabout vans, deliveries, their clusters of twig-nests, their births, marriages and deaths, independent of the tolling of bells or the architecture of spires; in their dark feathers the warrior eyes, the fluctuant centuries, the millennia.

In the nuns' garden the sisters stand apart, so few now, they hold together in a cluster of dark-brown habits; they are shy birds on the shore of a fraught and pounding sea.

Though we have breached – Stations of the Cross on this Good Friday – their defences, we have little to do with the distances between us, little to do with the tongue's fidelity to silence, with the will's self-confining strength in a bare cell; we think of them as dead before they are dead.

In the furthest garden, like artificial flowers, small stone crucifixes outline short lives: Sister Benedict, for instance: postulant at sixteen, novice at eighteen, professed at twenty-one, dead at twenty two and buried here; buried in bridal gown and veil, a golden ring on her finger; over them all the delicate, persistent blossoms of the saxifrage.

The priest comes, scattering water over them, but it is we, at our stations, who turn, perplexed, back to the demands of family and festival, sustained by the still beating heart of the nuns' garden, of those who battled for us, offering testimony of love, self-sacrifice, and dream.

We may know the racing of thoroughbreds along wind-hardened sand, relish the challenges of the shopping mall, may savour gourmet food with a rare wine, and we walk, in praise and honour, on the good earth, but when the garden gate is locked at last, an aeon done, a story told and a language dying, where will be our stations?

* * *

By the proud and Persian-blue upshowing lupins I found the young song-thrush, its fawn and buff dark-speckled breast torn open, its naked claws twisted, and flies – that bottle-green metallic gloss along the back – gorging;

we will, this summer, miss a chorister.

Though you grow older and the years harden you, the variousness of grief and its great breadth do not diminish.

Suddenly the memory: of the landrail, its day-and-night persistent craeking, no music in it, like a monk head-down in the stalls, off-key during Lauds;

and days of the chiff-chaff and yellowhammer litanies, scythe-time, in the harmonious and plenteous long-ago;

and I remembered father, in days of hay-raking and haycock-making within secure frontiers of the small meadow, as he paused and, near-in-tune, sang out to us:

'Oh the days of the Kerry dances, gone alas like our youth, too soon.'

* * *

It is the time when kings go out to battle and I yet may see a sign down our blackberry lane, reading 'Men at War'.

Ten thousand crosses around the Temple Mount; Nazis, the Red Army, Israel's murder machine, Islamic State, Kim Jong-un, Donald Trump;

and, after the hurricanes of violence have been stilled, the women raped, the children will be flung onto the rubble-piles.

We do not yet know what we are, we know we are not what we must be.

We study the history books, war theories, volumes on the nature of humankind – we have not found out why there is such a will to violence and destruction: the way physicians flayed a man to learn the workings of his veins, until they found that he had died.

Today I watched the rain place diamond-drops on the soft leaves of the briars, then bright sunlight lifted the fruit into slight and shivering ecstasy.

* * *

The spread-out wings of the harvester, shivering on the wall, are miniature stained-glass windows; season's end, waiting; and God is sweet, the cosmos savoury, and dangerous.

Harvester, touching the mass of the unknown Nothingness.

Afternoon: I had arrived almost too late;

mother, propped up on her final pillows, did not know me, asking father, softly, who that fellow is, her eyes already seeing far beyond me.

Her going, such a slight breath, the slightest shivering, as if a small breeze passed, a tiny lift of the body and she was not.

I kissed her pastel-yellow brow, touched her sparse silver-grey and brushed-up hair; after the difficult, kempt years, what hurt me most was the long-limbed bobby hairpin hanging loose. Undone.

* * *

Clouds were thunder-dark, crowding the sky; all else was stillness, as if waiting;

I heard a sudden shrill cry, as of a child, articulate without meaning, above the brooding cityscape;

I thought a voice beyond the darkness might have learned the answer to the mystery of us, and I looked up;

five great birds were circling, high above, climbing an invisible spiral and drifting eastwards, towards the sea: buzzards, alien birds, with one raw rook diving at them;

where I stood, herons were mating high in the canopy of an oak, shuddering the branches, shrieking their commitment to the being of heron, parading the gawky and gaunt elegant ugliness of their flight.

World stressed and urgent, its energies in constancy, where we were aliens and pilgrims, one now with the flow of the river, the yellow eel, the kingfisher, the gentle taking of hands through the long, darkening night.

* * *

On the wall, over the dead fireplace in the upstairs bedroom, as a child I was faced with this picture: a woman, a man, a child, and over them a bird, stylized, silver-bright, static, with wings spread;

at night, when a car passed on the road outside, heading across the island towards Keel, headlights lifted over the small meadow and drifted like a ghost across the wall, startling that bird with its light.

Years later, as I began to understand, I stood on a low headland, just over the beach where the Atlantic Ocean comes pounding, learning of its perpetual motion, waves turning and returning through all the nights and days;

Killeen – I learned of a womb-life that was too short, and the darkness too long, of a birth that was a matter of pain, and the burial secret;

and I imagined:

folded, unnamed, in a hardwood toolbox, the boy whose ears had never heard the waves, whose eyes had never watched a gannet move across the sky in silver-white beauty and power, a boy who was not forgotten but never spoken of, save in the silence and timelessness of sorrow;

and later still I learned more about You, the Comforter, the Advocate, the most withdrawn, the giver of seven gifts.

You, secretive, in bird-disguise, mourning, collared, fire in breast and tongue;

You, the unseen thread between word and word, breath and breeze, over-shadower and shuffler in the thunderbreak, the unheard wing-beat disturbing air;

scarlet light in the disrobing of the Christ;

mystery beyond mystery, beloved beyond all loving.

ON YOUR BIRTHDAY

I have found with you that peace and kind
that I have long sought, the fullness that swells

in the certainty that I have loved, and love,
am loved. I think of the first, uninhibited

chapters of Genesis, the gasp of Creation,
the first movement of the symphony, from

skittering wren in the shrubbery, to archaeopteryx
lumbering among the planets, of the bright-eyed joy

of the Child-God as he rolled out the thunder
of his laughter. The exuberant redcurrant bush

has streamers of scarlet fruit like lustrous
Christmas baubles and I sing a canticle in my heart,

to you and to my Christ, of clay and berry, and wonder
why on earth we are not perpetually singing.

* * *

I touch again the small hard beads of remembering – ways into the quietly-humming machinery of the heart: moonlight over Altamira, the high swell of the ocean off the beach, Aegina. You.

There is the thumbprint of love on the bread you bake, the rambunctious history of Rome in the spelt grain.

I relish the munificence of our marriage, and how we know the most mundane and intimate movements of one another's days, all of it sacrament, that you and I may hold together beneath the high, blue canopy.

Let them shout out *Mazel Tov* and *Dia Libh* and I will smash a whiskey glass under my foot;

we will take hands and leap together over the twig, the besom, the broom that they have placed at an angle across the doorway, into the joy and feasting of togetherness.

We drove together to our wedding in the foothills of Dublin, in a small chapel, where I announced (and announce again) the greatness of the sun and moon, the wholeness of the mysteries, and your wondrous love.

for Ursula

* * *

We are standing high on the hills of Clare Island, and could be in a place where once was a legendary hill; where continents shift, where mountains fall away.

Atlantic spirits now drift about the fallen God-stones; the salted winds find temporary residency, amongst the sweet and dangerous scent of nettles.

In this space centuries gone, the sun flared on a raised chalice, tongues gently touched with the melting bread of a grand passion, prayers were raised into the winds like keening.

I looked out, through the broken wall, to a patch of sunlight lying like a stole upon the island; the grassy shore is wet in places, and treacherous, reed-beds, water-hens, a lapwing, slough, quagmire, bog;

there is the ongoing struggle with demons within, the lost years, migrations, returns, the ever-present need for forgiveness, of self and others.

Quiet now – here you are alone, though the spirits surround you – listen for the ferns unfurling, for the whisperings of the shy violet; watch for the gannet's beautiful and terrifying flight over the sea.

There will be mountains again, there will be light, a lasting peace, abundant love.

All that I have learned is what my poems let me know.

*   *   *

I see her still, girl-child, on the golden strand, Atlantic Ocean at her back and she is kneeling as if intent at prayer, building;

bucket and spade are rainbow-coloured, a stream from the mountain shapes a moat about her castle;

the sky is azure-pure and at ease;

how the heart, watchful, swells with love and strains towards her, to hold her ever in protection.

Because the years will pass, without return, unlike the tides, and there come storms to be braced against, to stand hand in hand beside another.

Elsewhere, beyond island, I see the boy-child, knee-high to the iris, moving awed among rainbow-coloured fields, while bees – humming multitudes of them – are harvesting against the future.

I marvel, as I do when night comes like a high schooner under sail, stars at the masthead and beautiful from bow to stern – I marvel at the mystery that has brought two souls together, at the inadequacy of words save that rainbow-coloured one: love.

Because the years will pass, without return, unlike the tides or daffodils, and there come storms to be braced against, and they are standing hand in hand beside one another.

for Laura and Jeroen

THE WORLD IS CHARGED

I was startled by the squawk, the simultaneous
long-tailed and spread-winged half-spectacular half-dive

of the cock-pheasant, his wattles, his bronzed body
up over the hedge; and see! there! the Japanese anemone,

pea-green heart within a scatter-ring of gold; and here –
humbler still, and local – see the mares-tail weed

and the quick reaching of the briars, look, too, how the tiny
pimpernel persist along the driveway, from the red gate

to the back door; astonishment, from heart to eye to ragwort,
from there to woodlouse, eucalyptus, owl, and on to Sirius

and the Plough… And we have been, years, she and I,
walking by fields where generations lived and loved,

have laboured and have disappeared – with their sheds
and implements and cattle – into the deep, where they stay

resonant in their silence, their poorer cottages crumbled
into the liqueur of rose hips, the dust of nettles, knowing we too

will be with them, alive and loving in the warm light
that still persists, hereabouts, and everywhere, and forever.

* * *

I walked, steeped in grace, by old high walls and a garrisoned gate that had kept the gentry safe from the rude corruption without;

I could see a lightly wooded area, scarecrow trees with white-flesh bark;

and walking figures, not walking, merely slow motion, forwards, backwards, willing to meld with trees or find themselves at rest again, underground, or tableted to relative oblivion.

Big House, relict, hushed of its grand pianos and black-suited quartets, salons quartered into cells, with one-way peep-holes to watch from this world into a next.

At night, a restless quiet – and up there the stars, rock-dead in the great vast.

How they might cherish the comfort of a mist of unknowing;

how lives, (and such they are) seem wasted, questions of luck, genetics, inferiority, the demons within.

When they go, out of the demesne of time, and into eternal groves, I ask – what of the mind, Lord? what of the mind?

There are shimmering webs on the morning bushes
like the fine-silk net on granny's greying hair;

sorrow had made her body weightier; she sat,
dressed in black, under the heavy-scented

clambering rose, hands folded in her lap, life
having brought her to a taut quietness. Aged,

she would not have known, in those Catholic years,
of the eros of tree and flower, yearning, like us

for the wholeness of being. In pages of the *Irish Press*
she wrapped away green Bramley apples for the winter,

the kitchen scented with the sweet-sour aroma
of her baking. I see her now as a well-appointed

country chapel, Our Lady of the Wayside, and all
is mast and husk in the world, all memory and loss.

MAGPIE

On the high branches of the ash, a magpie sways
with the breeze, scolding in a voice

hoarse as the wauling of a tom-cat, her screech
salted with the blood of sparrow-chick and carrion;

she is urging her brood to be denizens of sky and earth,
of a world cherishing of all its citizens. It is good,

this afternoon, to be lying low on the Li-Lo, relishing
the wafted scent of the climbing rose, while robin,

that cheeky charmer, filches the ripening raspberries.
This is Ireland, and island, for centuries saturated with belief,

the monks, the monasteries, the long-enduring faithful,
clinging, too, to the beauty of earth, passionately

clinging, though the seas go on rising
ever higher against us, and the corporations waul.

* * *

A solitary heron, big against the darkening sky, passed, in rickety slow flight above the streetlamps, bearing cold and singleness across the city – while rook and gull, black inkblots under leaden clouds, flew high, disordered, towards their roosts.

Morning will bring again the reading in the papers of yesterday's death columns.

Ein jeder Engel, Rilke wrote, *ist schrecklich*;

and do the angels fly, late and late, across the black night sky, to roost, leaving their charges that have yielded themselves to vehemence, to stir fitfully in their sleep?

And do such souls turn dark as the sable back-guard of the mirror, the God turning away, unable to see himself in closed eyes, while they consign themselves to annihilation?

There are those who live out long and comfortable days
in spiritual squalor; but at times I will remember the large

hydrangea bush where a slow rain came dripping down
off purple lace-cap blooms onto dark grass

and the sound the falling made was like spirits whispering;
my grannie wept, soundlessly, over her handsome son

who worked in black-grease engine-rooms of merchant ships
tossed about on unpacific seas and her tears appeared to me

to be purple flower-petals falling; mother told of her beautiful
sister Patricia who died, too young, and how she turned back

for a final kiss before the dying; Patricia, godmother, had held me
in an off-white lace-work shawl, over the baptismal font

to cleanse away dark waters. I watch our baby learn the world
piece by piece by putting it in his mouth, and I will tell him, later,

how I failed, after trying several years, to determine the savour
of my Christ by dressing myself in black and urging tears.

* * *

Evening, I was driving on the wind-swept meadow-bogs of Erris when, at the first turn, a cock-pheasant crossed, making a procession of himself in his mitre-and-chasuble male finery; the heathers were a darkening lilac amongst green-marsh shallows and igloo clamps of turf; a mist came passing, like a whispering of pilgrims, and all the bogs seemed gentle-hearted as if, out here, the spirit was brooding still over creation.

It is said that God made humans in his likeness but we – are we worth more than sparrows? more than the cleg, than the mosquito or the tic-in-the-grass?

A badger, crushed, lay in roadside dust, abandoned like a ripped-up tyre; I stopped to edge it off the road into the ditch – already an under-earth stench of rot and darkness assailed me; out on the plains of Erris I felt how we, humans, are invasive, threatening and violent, and will be one – in time – with all the dust; night, and black whip-chord clouds were slicing the pale half-moon in strips, and my headlights caught the night-fox as she – leisurely, queenly – crossed before me, this cautious Bedouin of the boglands, one with us in our necessary predations, steel-grey as a wolf, eyes dull-white in the moonlight; Teach us, Christ-Fox, I prayed, how to live, to care and take care, to be spirit in the spirit-scape, to be whole.

I CONFESS

that there are white white butterflies alighting
on the white white Shasta daisies; between

the dill and the fuchsia there's a spider-thread
with light darting across it and back again like

little silver eels. Mid-afternoon, and high above,
drift the dark-grey, grey-black, black and

lethargic clouds with – just underneath – flight
of the white and soaring almost translucent

common gull bringing the darkness to light,
the drabness to animation. *Contemptus mundi*

they taught us, how to renounce loveliness,
to cower indoors one's reductive self, to kneel

in boxed, tobacco-scented darkness and confess
original sins, to hoard up selfishly treasure in heaven.

SEA SALT

He was walking unsteadily now, as if on a sloping
deck; they had to fix a handrail to his bathroom wall;

you could cry to see him, stubble on his face
as stiff, fierce and salty as lichens on sea-rocks.

Near full ebb, he'd say, when you'd ask.
His old house had sea-shells of all shapes and colours

fixed in the plaster so he could sit within a storm
and hear the ocean tell of the cosmic powers

and the rough rocky-shore edging of his God.
When I visited, I found him in a nursing home,

among old landlubbers who could scarcely
stand on the floorboards of the wards. The sea floor

is slicked, he told me, for ballroom dancing,
but they'll bury me deep in mouldy earth for ever.

* * *

For a time the green of the lawn stayed green, but the hedge beyond, and the trees beyond that, the hill in the distance and the trees on the ridge of the hill were all black, sharply outlined against the sky, while clouds of a variousness of greys and blue-greys and a small streak of a weakly washed-pink colour quickly turned to black

and the lawn grew dark as the sky, and suddenly – though it was not suddenly – it was night while I was trying to reason within myself about the dreadful ongoing wars, of the mindful yet mindless violence more rampant than ever in this our new and most enlightened century,

how, once, I dreamed – like Israel – of the vengeance of the justice of Yahweh, of the expectations of apocalypse, but had trust only in the hope of a healing, how the unblighted soul of the child could be restored after turpitude and could glow once more with the ease-filled restoration of light, the recovery of sights worth seeing, the raising of the dead from the devastations of the pit.

* * *

I sit a long time, inside glass, anticipating birds at the bird-table: robin, chaffinch, tit – but there is news of violence in the world; I am listening to the radio, Donizetti's *L'elisir d'amore*, but the words seem far and the dream foolish.

The noise of wars disrupts all harmony and I no longer find what was and is and was to be in the music, remembering how they let me loose at the piano, to learn scales and exercises, major-minor.

I wanted to be outside, fingering the real world, its ear-tests, its eye-tests, clear stream-water trilling over pebbled sand.

When I heard, in Santa Maria della Pietà, Vivaldi's *Seasons*, I thought that world and music had shivered into one,

until the vacant eyes of the slaughtered Christ disturbed me, as if Michelangelo had known the music of white marble and drew forth his Pietà, then, striking at the block, abandoned it.

HOME OF THE LOST

The loganberries, scarlet and plump, dissolve
like blood-hosts in the mouth; the loganberry bush

has been swallowed over by the trailing
branches of the sweet pea – rioting petals of blue

and pink and violet – and all of flesh is grass and dust
and cosmic gold. Winter hails already

in the noonday light, the fuzzball heads of the alium
have flourished away into air-light filaments

like the powdery hairs off-white on the dead man's breast.
I lie in wait to surprise the God in his being while magpies

clutter like waitresses at a function and cackle with mirth
on the chimney-pots. Nothing satisfies; there is too much

vastness and we are brooding over the failure of our little
hearts, unable to ground the mystery this side of death.

* * *

A young child, I mouthed the given words, gazing up at the modest reproduction of the icon: but found no comfort in the eyes – nor in the stylized dark-night-blue and gold-star threaded drapes and garments – Mother of Perpetual Succour.

The gaze of the teenage child-boy was turned away, towards winged angels in a brown sky and the words troubled me: 'succour' and 'perpetual', and the alien title, Icon, something eastern, and vaguely threatening.

What I loved was the pleasure I knew at being alone, scuffing my shoes on the wooden floor of the hay-loft where spillicles of hay still lifted in almost invisible hay-dust, making me sneeze, and I could relish the sounds of *me* happening in a world I alone inhabited.

Often, in the slow persistent rains shifting like wraiths across the fieldscapes of the west, I pressed my face against the window, suffering tedium, mother in the dark kitchen baking soda bread, the icon always watching, those long and sculpted fingers troubling, the eyes attentive, inquiring, broaching sorrow.

The woman watches still, though now I know her name, Miriam, her village, Nazareth, I know the flowers by her back door and how she baked her barley bread; now she is a presence for which I'm grateful, sensible of her care, her suffering, her un-reproachful eyes.

ONE THAT GATHERS SAMPHIRE
(King Lear)

And where, then, in your life, have you been?

Have been shifting a few sand-grains, dribbling
some drops of salt water. It has been as foam

at the sea's edge, soiled and shivering, held in the hands
a while, till the wind took it. I did not fit too well

into this world, slipping several times on the marble steps
before the altar. But I loved well, long and deeply,

buoyed up on the swell of it and touching ground,
finding at last sufficiency, there on the cliff-top,

staring over, watching down for the landing-place,
the harbour; I was, too, that minuscule figure

at the cliff's root, watching upward. I, too, translating
myself slowly into meaning. To find the ground

where pilgrimage ends, where pilgrimage begins, learning
the innocence of islands, the unruliness, the danger.

* * *

Evening in Cleggan;

articulated trucks are heavy with crates of crabs and lobsters raked from the liberal Atlantic; these, our fellow-predators, suffer immaculate pain.

The trucks move out into the night, red lights sketching a path across darkness;

soon it will be the forceful ferries in dim-lit ports, then the throb of engines over ocean forest floors, lobsters, their claws taped shut, scrambling in their water-tanks in a darkness within a darkness, and crabs, their slow sideways scurrying, their pop-eyes useless.

In the lounge, the truckers stretch and gossip, their thickening bodies shaken from roads and cobbles, from wave-rutted sea-lanes, inconstant waves;

but – there has always been lobster-flesh, picked out by a myriad thick fingers over the centuries, Rome, Alexandria, Ogunquit Maine – and here, sea's edge, white linen table-cloths, tall aristocratic candles – where we, too, are transients, ghosts of who we are yet to become.

* * *

Blue-tits, the chicks, came from the nest and hesitated on the edge of a high eve-chute, three of them, fluffed, edgy themselves and whimpery, beautiful, even in near-fledge, striking in glossy black caps, bright yellow bibs;

from somewhere the adults called – fling caution to the breeze, they sang, the air is soft and flight will be your wholeness, your deliverance;

so the first one fluttered out, stuttered, and flew;

a second slow-floated down onto the concrete patio, stumbled like an awkward skater, then flew low and fast into the shrubbery;

the third, the smallest, baby-chick, chic, and runt, hesitated, called, fluffed its gold and white feathers and fell, out of the gutter onto the hard ground;

stirred a little, stalled.

I buried it under the new shrub rose, beneath the wine-dark blooms, where it winters now, as the rose-bush winters.

I, too, made of the self-same star-dust, the same feathering.

AGAIN THE EUCALYPTUS

Out of nothing is love born, born barely half-
formed, formed slowly and merging into another

love, half-formed. I am writing this in a time of war,
there being never a time when there is not war;

for there is war in the fabric of the eucalyptus trees and
there is love in the leaves and health and presence

of the eucalyptus, love in the roots stirring and reaching
through the soil, love in the high soul-whispering. A tree

standing alone stands in sadness, its scattered seeds
bear only sorrow. The heart, too, is strange in its rhythms

and heavy in its isolation; and the heart is well aware
that everything has its seasons, a season for casting seeds,

a season for gathering. In the shadow of the eucalyptus
the thistle-thorny blackthorn bush displays a bountiful

offering of night-blue sloes, beautiful and bitter as human
promise and dismay. Real night coming on to weave its darkness

over all. I will crush the autumn leaves of the eucalyptus
between my fingers and offer you the harvest of their scent.

The Greek gods have hidden themselves away, despising us for our incredulity and littleness; in Crete, because they had been in love with islands, you may divine them, if you leave your old heart open.

And I could be one of the old gods now, stiff and gummy, red-rimmed about the eyes and hard of hearing; though once I was young, yesteryear and yesteryear, and teetered naked towards the pounding Atlantic water-walls;

but now, on the pebble beach at Plakias, I sat, unwilling to enter sea;

I folded my trousers to below my knees and paddled unsteadily in the gentle waves, then knew myself to be my aged father, awkwardly sitting on a stone attempting to dry my feet, draw on my socks, laboriously lift myself back up, and – staggering a little – stumble out over the brittle wrack and fragile leavings of the waves towards the car.

The gods are tongue-tied concerning their affairs but I have promised to honour them, as I honour the Christ who said it will be given to you at the time of need what you shall speak.

* * *

A flock of geese, Greenland white-fronted, came wheeling out of a dulled-black evening, cheering themselves shrilly towards their goal;

father's shot brought one slewing lewdly down in a flue of wings and feathers to shatter in the ice-logged bog.

The day of Myra's burial, they released white doves over the grave to find their way, northwards, to their cotes, as though they might ferry grief away into the distance.

A peacock, tense in extortionate beauty, parades his need inside the walled garden; in the cages loud with macaws and parakeets, exotic love birds tangle bills;

children watch, poking fingers through the mesh, while the wide blue sky scarce holds a cloud.

The human heart sometimes can scarcely hold its yearning; words like love, like loss, do not contain it, psalms and poems soar and swerve around it.

Our awed, most plangent prayers, rise at their best as not much more than a sigh, all of us creatures, under the same sky, the same impulse, the same song.

NOVEMBER

The old iron gate grates in rusty lassitude
protesting its forcing open. No

vacancies; fully occupied. Here is an acre plus
of drumlin land, soil richly damp

along the hollows, montbretia
fecund across the bottoms. But it is easy

to find wonder here, at the loveliness
of grass, the snake-reach of briars

with berries rancid under rain;
in higher reaches, earth is dry, plastic flowers

pale and waiting, like Mrs Haversham in *Great
Expectations*. Only the present matters. Still they come,

the dead, in delicacy, into our dreams, offering
bouquets of memory, white lilies of encouragement.

* * *

I will have known the edgy festival of the poem, attempts to touch hard facts of the immediate and play a plausible music, seeking what is beyond the facts and features, beyond processes of was, and is, and will-be.

To speak of the small crack across the glass face of the carriage clock – meaning a sorrow held in the long silence of an old country house.

Someday there will be the final lines, the last words set down, complete, and incomplete; poems, like leaves, free to wander in the breeze that takes them, carrying their burdens, their harvests.

I will have prayed: Spare me Lord for my days fall like rubble; what is man that you should magnify him, why do you tender towards him your heart of love? The light burns dimly, fingers fidget on the sheets; today I will lie down in dust, and if tomorrow you come in search of me, I am no more.

The darkness will be long. The lustre of black hair will not be seen as vanity.

Day darkens at the windows; it is a strain to walk uphill, there is constant danger of falling. Yet the crocus is in bloom, and the cherry-tree a mess of blossoms.

Mourners are gathering in the forecourt and the priceless ceramic jug has fallen off the shelf.

There is no vanity in the writing of your books, for everything will be brought out into searing light